Iranian Feminism
and Transnational Ethics
in Media Discourse

Iranian Feminism and Transnational Ethics in Media Discourse

Sara Shaban

LEXINGTON BOOKS
Lanham • Boulder • New York • London

Published by Lexington Books
An imprint of The Rowman & Littlefield Publishing Group, Inc.
4501 Forbes Boulevard, Suite 200, Lanham, Maryland 20706
www.rowman.com

86-90 Paul Street, London EC2A 4NE

British Library Cataloguing in Publication Information Available

Library of Congress Cataloging-in-Publication Data

Names: Shaban, Sara, 1988- author.
Title: Iranian feminism and transnational ethics in media discourse / Sara Shaban.
Description: Lanham, Maryland : Lexington Books, 2021. | Includes bibliographical
    references and index. | Summary: "Iranian Feminism and Transnational Ethics in
    Media Discourse explores how U.S. news and social media discourse hierarchies
    overshadow transnational feminist politics and reinforce femonationalist narratives,
    thereby unpacking how protesters' voices on the ground are obscured in favor of elite
    sources who reaffirm U.S Islamophobia"— Provided by publisher.
Identifiers: LCCN 2021039662 (print) | LCCN 2021039663 (ebook) |
    ISBN 9781793647269 (cloth) | ISBN 9781793647283 (paperback) |
    ISBN 9781793647276 (epub)
Subjects: LCSH: Muslim women—Iran—Social conditions. | Women—Iran—Social
    conditions. | Women—Political activity—Iran. | Women's rights—Religious
    aspects—Islam—Press coverage. | Feminism—Iran. | Islamophobia—Western
    countries. | Journalistic ethics—Western countries. | Social media and journalism.
Classification: LCC HQ1735.2 .S5 2021 (print) | LCC HQ1735.2 (ebook) |
    DDC 305.420955—dc23
LC record available at https://lccn.loc.gov/2021039662
LC ebook record available at https://lccn.loc.gov/2021039663

Contents

Acknowledgments

First and foremost, I would like to thank my doctoral adviser, Dr. Cristina Mislán, for her support, inspiration, and encouragement throughout my journey through the doctoral program. Her enthusiasm and passion for social justice motivated me to pursue an academic career as a critical/cultural scholar, and I am incredibly thankful to have her as my mentor and friend. She continues to push me to produce my best work and not to be afraid of my own voice.

I would also like to thank the members of my dissertation committee, Dr. Fritz Cropp, Dr. Joe Hobbs, Dr. Ryan Thomas, and Dr. Yong Volz. Dr. Cropp invested in my potential and enabled me to travel and learn from some of the greatest scholars in Middle Eastern studies and communication. He continues to encourage and remind me that anything is possible. Dr. Hobbs cultivated my love for the MENA region and mentored me as I learned to maneuver the scholarship surrounding Middle Eastern geopolitics. Dr. Thomas was always kind enough to sit and listen to my ideas for this or that project and helped me explore the concept of global journalism and how it can most ethically and effectively be implemented. Dr. Yong Volz is the epitome of a woman scholar in journalism, and I am grateful to have her as a mentor.

Completing a PhD program is not easy. I am thankful to my colleagues and very best of friends who supported and encouraged me throughout my academic journey: Courtney, Ciera, Joe, Erika, Ayleen, and Rachel. Thank you to my parents, Mohammed and Marie, for the on-call support. Finally, a huge thank you to my incredible life partner, Taylor, for his patience, encouragement, love, and support. I wouldn't be here without you.

Introduction

In late 2017, protests in Iran erupted against the government due to the government's dramatic increase in oil prices resulting from U.S. sanctions on Iranian oil exports. Within those larger protests was a different campaign, unassociated with the widely circulated government protests. Viva Movahed stood on a utility box in downtown Tehran to protest against the country's compulsory hijab law. Movahed's image was circulated via social media, and she became the unofficial symbol of the movement #WhiteWednesdays. #WhiteWednesdays is an online campaign featuring women from Iran, Saudi Arabia, Afghanistan, and others posting photos and videos of themselves either wearing a white scarf or nothing on their heads at all to show solidarity with other women protesting against compulsory hijab (Alinejad, 2018). While women in neighboring countries showed support, there was a questionable silence from Western feminists, most notably from women like Linda Sarsour, organizers of the women's march, and the Swedish prime minister who wore a hijab on her most recent visit to Iran. There was some speculation that the absence of a response from Western feminists was rooted in their loyalty to Obama's decision to join the Nuclear Deal with Iran—especially since the deal was predominantly negotiated by women, including U.S. Undersecretary of Political Affairs, Wendy Sherman (Kianpour, 2015). Additionally, some journalists suggested that Western feminists did not want to appear Islamophobic, particularly while they are working to normalize hijab in their own countries—consequently making up for their false pretenses for supporting Muslim women in the past.

Right-wing, conservative journalists took advantage of this silence and began to control the Western narrative surrounding #WhiteWednesdays, almost, if not, by default. These journalists began to criticize Western feminists by highlighting the bravery of women in Iran who risk imprisonment or death by publicly removing their hijabs. Furthermore, self-described Trump supporters and right-wing nationalists from the United States, the United Kingdom, and Canada began to cultivate a femonationalist discourse on Twitter. Femonationalism is a term created by Sara Farris (2017) that describes rhetoric utilizing feminist and gender equality language to promote anti-Islamic and xenophobic campaigns, usually practiced by right-wing, conservative Westerners. For example, some right-wing, conservative journalists used their platforms to weaponize Iranian women who are flogged for "bad hijab" to demonize hijabi women in the United States, like Linda Sarsour, who claim hijab as a form of freedom. This discourse assumes a singular definition of hijab and what it stands for while neglecting the transnational context of hijab (Hasan, 2018).

For decades, journalists have used the bodies of Muslim women throughout the Middle East, North Africa, and Central and South Asia in media coverage as a catalyst for orientalist narratives. However, the increasing population of Muslim women residing in the Western world within this age of globalization demands a change in discourse. Muslim women have been wrongfully portrayed as victims of Islam and Muslim men without acknowledging the very real persecution they face within the Western world. With the help of native informants and geopolitical agendas, journalists continue to perpetuate dangerous narratives regarding Muslim women. Such narratives can and have led to femonationalist rhetoric within the United Kingdom, France, Italy, and the United States, which, subsequently, cultivates ethnonationalism as well as a culture of fear and hate toward Muslims. The chapters in this book explore the dangers of femonationalist rhetoric present within news media coverage of Muslim women, specifically Iran, and how that coverage hurts Muslim women rather than working on their behalf. Traditional journalistic practices like objectivity and government sourcing play a large part in this issue. But not all is lost. By adopting a transnational feminist framework for journalism, the multifaceted truth surrounding Muslim women all over the world can more aptly be explored, and ethnocentric discourse can be challenged within journalism coverage. The eight chapters in this book argue for a more ethical and effective way of representation.

The first chapter explores the relationship between journalistic inquiry and globalization as well as what that means for the quality of news coverage on Muslim women. Since globalization permeated the media sphere, there has been a decline in resources for journalists all over the world, including the closure of foreign bureaus, a reliance on freelance writers, and extensive time constraints with higher production expectations. As resources deteriorate, inevitably, so does the quality of journalism. This is especially evident when covering international news, particularly when the event is loaded with contextual elements that rely on culture, history, and politics—for example, feminism in Muslim countries. The lack of context and conflicts of interest embedded in Western news coverage of Muslim women is a result of the neoliberal underpinnings cultivated by globalization in the realm of media. The process of globalization aims to consolidate people around the world into a single society that engages with a universal logic. In this case, that process would include the implementation of a ubiquitous form of journalism. Establishing a universal practice of journalism is problematic and fails to recognize the complexity of how different issues among nation states differ in geographical, political, and cultural contexts and, therefore, are affected in significantly different ways.

Furthermore, charting a global framework for journalism requires someone to establish the structure of that framework. Given the Western world's domination of journalism in both practice and scholarship, there lies the danger of implementing an imperialistic paradigm. However, by pursuing a more ecumenical approach to journalism, perhaps reporters can begin to recognize the gaps within different nation states' frames of reference. A transnational feminist framework can enable more equitable news coverage, especially when reporting on women's issues around the world.

Many Muslim women have responded to the Western mainstream news media's flawed reporting and its inability to capture the nuances within feminism in the Muslim world—not to mention the suppression of voices from the ground. Muslim women have taken to alternative media platforms to make their voices heard on a global scale. Chapter 2 explores both transnational feminism and alternative-activist new media by breaking down the elements of each concept and how those two concepts intersect. Specifically, the chapter explores Muslim women's involvement in social movements utilizing social media while also arguing against technological fetishism—granting technology more power than it actually has (Fuchs, 2012). Additionally, this chapter works through the different ways that Western media have othered Muslims through orientalist and neo-orientalist narratives.

To fully understand how Western mainstream news media disappointed women throughout the Muslim world, particularly Iran, it is imperative to determine the historical context between feminism and women in Iran. Chapter 3 traces Iranian women's participation—and often leadership—in social movements throughout Iran starting in 1848 through 2020. Iranian women could be found in campaigns advocating for nationalism and protesting imperialism—including the 1953 coup staged by the CIA against Iran's elected Prime Minister Mohammed Mossadegh. Recognizing many Iranian women's objections to imperialism is imperative to the conversation on transnational feminism. Feminists in Western countries have made efforts to stand in solidarity with Muslim women without understanding some of the problematic elements of those efforts. Chapter 3 specifically addresses women in the United States protesting the Islamic revolution in 1979 as well as the 2019 Christchurch mosque shootings in New Zealand where women wore scarves on their heads to demonstrate their solidarity with Muslims.

Western journalists did not necessarily come to these problematic representations of Muslim women on their own. With the help of native informants—those individuals who weaponize their lived experiences as a "native" to help perpetuate Islamophobic narratives—Western politicians and news outlets alike can utilize the rhetoric of those sharing negative experiences with Islam. Some of these include Ayaan Hirsi Ali, Bernard Lewis, and Fouad Ajami—all of whom have served their Western governments in international affairs with Muslim countries. Chapter 4 considers the role of Masih Alinejad in the Trump administration and her position within the U.S. government-funded news station Voice of America as well as how she started as an activist before evolving into an adviser to the U.S. government on Iranian affairs. Additionally, this chapter introduces Sara Farris' (2017) theoretical concept of femonationalism—the utilization of feminist or gender equality language to promote Islamophobic or xenophobic agendas—and its threat against both women and Muslims around the world.

Now, why does this matter? Sometimes, the gravity of a situation cannot be grasped until it hits close to home. In this case, the news coverage of the #WhiteWednesdays movement in Iran served as a springboard for femonationalist rhetoric that not only threatens people in Iran but also Muslims living in the Western world. With the help of native informants, journalists have relied on "official" sources from the government and have rarely reached out to grassroots voices that can easily be accessed via Twitter. Chapters 5, 6, and 7 use the White Wednesdays campaign as a case study to compare the narratives between mainstream U.S. news media and Iranians on Twitter—specifically Iranian women to help determine the gaps in discourse regarding Iran, Islam, and feminism.

The final chapter takes the results of the case study and asks how American journalists can reexamine the current paradigm in journalism that privileges official sources and ignores marginalized voices. Chapter 8 argues for a change in framework that includes more collaboration with grassroots activists on Twitter as well as an adoption of transnational journalism ethics. By embracing more non-conventional ways of knowing—like marginalized voices on social media—while practicing journalism in a way that actively considers people outside of the reporting country, journalism can begin to grow closer to more ethical and effective ways of representing Muslims, women, and activists all over the world.

Chapter 1

Globalization, Media, and Journalism

The intersection between neoliberalism and mainstream news media is key to understanding the future of global or transnational journalism. Neoliberalism, introduced in the 1980s, is a compilation of national/international policies for businesses and, consequently, social relations. Additionally, neoliberalism promotes universality on an economic level as well as a specific ideology and lifestyle (Dardot and Laval, 2013), including individualization, independence, and the privatization of public services like energy, water, and education. The neoliberal framework eventually evolved into the practice of privatizing public services, disdain for government programs (i.e., welfare and Medicaid), and the promotion of capitalism. Essentially, neoliberalism in the Western world became equated with modernization—with the goal of permeating the rest of the world with this newfound paradigm for living. The modern paradigm became a homogenizing process that placed Western society as the gold standard for societies all over the world (Tipps, 1976).

Neoliberalism is closely related to globalization—especially when it comes to media. Globalization is the process of incorporating people across the globe into a single society (Albrow, 1990). These global connections started with finance and entertainment before branching into journalism. The intersection between journalism and globalization originated with global media corporations calling for a global journalism, similar to the efforts made by advertising and entertainment industries (Reese, 2010). Media scholars have defined global journalism in a variety of ways, with Reese (2010) interpreting it as a "global public sphere" borrowing from McLuhan's (1967) "global village." This idea of a global public sphere involves transnational logic and unitary media/journalistic form. Ideally, it would "create politically significant spaces" engaging different publics; however, realistically, these transnational connections "privilege certain forms of power" and appeal to an elite audience. For example, consider the original forms of "transnational media"—*International Herald Tribune, Wall Street Journal Europe*, and *The Financial Times*. These outlets are primarily finance-focused and rooted in Western countries, highlighting the relationship between globalization and the economic sector before working its way into international relations, sociology, cultural studies, and history. Yet, if global journalism is meant to reflect McLuhan's (1967) "global village," then the media have failed to achieve this vision and instead embody a more "glocal" approach, projecting world news as it applies to the local community rather than the world. In contrast, the global village suggests "a homogeneity of world views," or "a diverse 'dialog of cultures'" (346). But the global media system of the twenty-first century does not reflect this globalization largely because domestic interests tend to reign over global ones—which is not the goal of journalists. There is this expectation that there should be a universal logic that creates a ubiquitous form of journalism that would eventually cultivate a global public sphere. However, practicing a generic form of journalism would be a disservice to the global audience.

Because news media has proved unsuccessful at implementing a universal practice, one might ask what hinders the assimilation process. For one, theoretical global news networks like "CNN International" and "BBC World News" do not have a truly global reach (stories are not translated into multiple languages; foreign news caters to elitist populations). Neither do these "global" networks appear to significantly differ from any other international report. This is especially problematic because international reporting has historically been characterized as lacking context and playing into conflicts of interest. Instead of enlarging the space for a nuanced narrative, international reporting is often rooted in "home-grown" narratives that tell a "substantially different story" than other national news networks (Hafez, 2009). For example, news coverage of the Iraq war in 2003 varied depending on the news network's perspective and geographical location. Western news networks would focus on "weapons of mass destruction" while another would push "American imperialism" (327). Reasons for this differing coverage could result from journalists' lack of cultural context or international education, language barriers when recruiting sources, the decline of foreign correspondents, government propaganda, or a reliance on serving a domestic audience rather than an international one (Hafez, 2009). Even the widely acclaimed CNN World News produces stories with a nationalist or ethnocentric slant to an audience with a similar world view.

That said, establishing the practice of global journalism with a universal network, message, and audience, is nearly, if not completely, impossible. However, by attempting to pursue such a feat, journalists can recognize the gaps in different nation states' frames of reference (Reese, 2010). By acknowledging these disparities in reporting, news networks can look toward improving a "cross-national awareness of events" (348) in a world continually shaped by globalized institutions and pursue transnational journalism.

JOURNALISM ETHICS

Global media ethics is an admirable goal, if not slightly unrealistic. Given the realities of colonialism and globalization, a universal code of ethics is unattainable, especially regarding women's issues across the world. However, a shift away from the concept of global media ethics toward a transnational framework is a conceivable goal and one that should apply to news coverage on women's issues in the Middle East. The practical and ethical differences between global and transnational journalism must be addressed to explore this transnational framework.

Global journalism is a difficult concept to define and even more challenging to operationalize. But that has not kept media scholars from trying. The concept of global journalism rests on the theory that news cannot simply be placed in confined categories like "local," "national," and "international"—especially with events and crises like climate change or COVID-19, which are clearly global issues (Berglez, 2008). Global journalism represents "the world as a unified body" where a particular event can simultaneously affect the world (850). Additionally, global journalism can produce content that illustrates connections between events that occur on a local or domestic level to a global plane (Van Leuven and Berglez, 2016). While global journalism's theoretical aspect makes sense, the actual practice would be challenging for journalists to implement effectively.

In the words of media ethicist Stephen Ward (2005), "with global reach comes global responsibility" (p. 5). Ward recognized the effects of globalization on media corporations and, subsequently, their influence on news media, calling for a reinterpretation of journalism ethics, particularly through a cosmopolitan point of view or, what Berglez calls, a global outlook. A cosmopolitan journalist is "a journalist who is connected with stakeholders in other countries and works to connect her audience to a global public sphere and who shares the normative presuppositions of a global media ethics" (Lindell and Karlsson, 2016, 868). This ethical approach is based on credibility, justifiable consequence, and humanity. On this last point on humanity, Ward (2005) elaborates on the duties of journalism with a global outlook, challenging journalists to act as global agents, serve world citizens, and enhance nonparochial understandings. Globalization, coupled with the idea of "global" journalism, calls on journalists to serve audiences across the world, ranging in different cultural, economic, and geographical contexts.

PUTTING THEORY INTO PRACTICE

Empirically, Berglez (2008) suggests that analyzing the following journalistic representations of space, power, and identity can identify characteristics of global journalism:

> Space: In what ways and to what extent is there a multifaceted geography in which journalism interrelates processes and practices simultaneously occurring in separate places worldwide? Power: In what ways and to what extent are topics and conflicts explained as a complex mixture of domestic, foreign, and global powers? Identity: In what ways and to what extent does news journalism cross national and continental borders when representing (political) identities? (854)

When conceptualizing what it means to be "global," there is an expectation that this would encapsulate the entire world (Reese, 2010). When you couple the concept of global with "journalism" (the practice, the institution, or the concept), one can assume that this journalism refers to and affects the whole world through a global perspective. A global perspective requires a global network of journalists producing global work (in various languages) reaching a global audience (Hellmueller et al., 2017; Lindell and Karlsson, 2016). A universal standard of objectivity, ethics, and ideology must be established to achieve this goal.

In a study analyzing the news practices at BBC World News, Dencik (2013) conducted several interviews with journalists on their own global news practices based on Berglez's (2008) "global outlook." Dencik (2013) asked BBC journalists how they differentiate between coverage for a domestic outlet versus a global outlet. The majority of the interviewees did not recognize any significant differences between domestic and global outlets and mentioned that any amendments made to news reports to take them from a domestic to a global level story are merely cosmetic. This perspective was based on two primary ideas: (1) BBC World News journalists consider Britain to be a "cosmopolitan society," meaning news reports are always "covered with a global outlook" and (2) any international news coverage broadcasted to a British audience would be produced in a way that is accessible to an audience "unfamiliar with the local context" (128). Additionally, the interviewees suggested that foreign news does not always interest domestic audiences but rather appeals to a more elitist population with a broader worldview than the average person. By assuming an elitist audience for foreign news coverage, BBC World News journalists assume that their standard reporting style is already global in terms of broadcasting to a globally minded audience.

Within this same study, Dencik (2013) also addressed the danger of reconceptualizing the idea of global journalism into a term that excuses important aspects of what it means to be global. She poses the following question: Who are the global citizens, and whose moral global order points the direction for global journalism? Dencik's question goes beyond issues of imperialism and confronts the power structures that dictate how globalization influences news media. Assuming what it means to be global without undertaking the research necessary to defining globality allows for existing power structures to illegitimately claim to be global. Meaning, news media outlets must be careful to claim a global identity if their normative practices suggest otherwise.

So, what do the normative practices of global journalism look like? Van Leuven and Berglez (2016) take Berglez's (2013) model featuring space, power, and identity, to task in an empirical study examining three domestic newspapers from France, Germany, and Poland. The authors seek to operationalize global journalism based on Berglez's model pertaining to complex relations while also introducing this new element of reader engagement techniques. Reader engagement techniques are described as "news media's ability to clearly illuminate and actively demonstrate the reality of globalization and its impact on people's everyday lives" (671), very similar to the way foreign correspondents domesticate international news for their home audiences. These engagement techniques are measured by (a) involvement ("how news audiences are potentially part of a global problem"); (b) concreteness ("the extent news media relate global conditions to people's everyday lives"); and (c) inescapability ("the extent to which news media portray global crises and issues as social conditions that cannot be easily suppressed or avoided") (671–672). The study revealed that domestic news was dominant though "glocalized" news was also prevalent. Van Leuven and Berglez (2016) concluded that while global journalism practices are not yet normative, the potential still exists and can be better established through further empirical study.

In a similar vein, Lindell and Karlsson (2016) use Ward's (2005) global journalism ethics theory along with Beck's (2006) concept of "cosmopolitanism." Lindell and Karlsson (2016) operate on the assumption that the role of a global journalist is to reject parochial narratives and "connect citizens of the world to a global public sphere" (p. 860). Under this assumption, the authors conducted a study on Swedish journalists and their implementation of global journalism principles (Ward, 2005) while also testing to see if the journalists supported the idea of making those principles normative. Based on Berglez (2008) and Ward's (2005, 2010) understanding of global journalism, the authors operationalized the concept as involving: (a) working with global or transnational issues, (b) connecting audiences to a global public sphere, and (c) promoting non-parochial understandings (p. 863). Additionally, Lindell and Karlsson (2016) made a note of the journalists' contact with citizens in other countries as well as their ability to connect their audiences "to the world as a whole" (p. 863). The authors found that while most of the journalists supported the principles of global journalism (Ward, 2005), they did not implement those principles regularly, if at all. Results also revealed that local community news is favored over EU and global issues and pushed by the hierarchy of the news network. And finally, journalists admitted that they consider their purpose to "primarily connect its audience to a local, and national, social body rather than the European Union and the world as a whole" (p. 864). The lack of global journalism implementation makes it difficult to measure empirically if it exists beyond the conceptual at all.

Another important aspect to consider in the operationalization of global journalism is the journalist herself. How do journalists realistically apply global framing in their story construction? The answer might be found within the global news start-up industry. Global news startups culminated in decreasing foreign correspondent jobs as some news organizations closed their international bureaus and relied on foreign freelancers instead. Through the global start-up model, foreign news became a commodity rather than a public service. The start-up itself serves as somewhat of an agent for different freelancers all over the world, connecting them with different clients including, *The New York Times, Al Jazeera, Australian Broadcasting Company*, and *The Sun*. In a study on global news startups, Hellmueller, Cheema, and Zhang (2017) interviewed editors and founders from eight of the "most established and well-known global news startup organizations" to determine the roles of global journalists as well as the values and economic principles established by those editors and founders.

The interviews revealed that while the global news startups are ideologically motivated, they are also driven by the liberal market as the startups are for-profit and serve as a more economical option for news organizations. Within this framework, the relationship between globalization and journalism is more focused on the capital to be gained rather than serving world citizens (Ward, 2005). The interviewees also revealed that most of their freelancers' (based in the United States, Europe, and Australia) work is published in English, given that their clients are mostly based in Western countries, except for Russia.

The authors also examined the freelancers' content to determine if it was reported from a global outlook. Ultimately, the majority of the stories were focused on geopolitics and terrorism. Additionally, the sources for these stories were predominantly from Western Europe and North America, with few coming from Western Asia. Little if any of the sources came from Central America, South America, Eastern Europe, Africa, or Eastern Asia. Note that the kinds of stories sourced from these areas included the 2015 Paris attacks, the ISIS threat, and the Syrian refugee crisis. While the news content featured a mix of national, transnational, and global events, the authors still found the global aspect of these foreign reports lacking. While the goal may be to provide stories that serve a global audience, the stories that these global news startups are producing are clearly written for a Western audience. Without incorporating stories in other languages, translating stories from other countries, and diversifying their sources, these journalists are far from being characterized as global.

The central tendencies for global journalism's conceptual and operational definitions are to simplify the concept into something measurable. While scholars admit that their empirical definition of the concept is lacking, they continue to shape the concept in a way that is convenient for their purposes. Essentially, the concept is vulnerable to manipulation by its handler. The different definitions, purposes, and variances for global journalism waiver between the semi-acceptable/more empirically feasible definition and the conceptually/empirically challenging one. A global journalism scale might include a basic level: cross-awareness of events, linking events from all over the world, examining how things are interrelated, and contextualizing transnational events/news, or, essentially, Berglez's (2008) global outlook. On a more extensive and authentic level, the concept might refer to Ward's (2005) definition of global journalism in all aspects (practically, ethically, etc.) in which journalists are synonymous with global agents and promote news that is reported from an international perspective, serving all world citizens, and working to engage in discourses that aim to help people worldwide understand each other.

CONCEPTUAL DEFINITION

While a global journalism framework is an ideal worth aspiring to, it is impractical and would require a global consensus on what global reporting should look like. As of now, the construction of that new paradigm is limited to Western scholarship, or to what Rao and Lee (2005) call the "postcolonial suspicion"—the concern that any discussion on global media ethics will prioritize Western interests. In the interim, journalists would do better to widen the space for more contextualized reporting and seek out original stories that allow for more criticism of varying perspectives and worldviews (Hafez, 2009). This practice can be characterized as transnational journalism. Transnational journalism offers a more approachable strategy to both ethically and effectively report on issues at every level (i.e., local, national, international, or global). Some scholars have used transnational journalism and global journalism interchangeably (Berglez, 2007; Hellmueller, 2017), but they are not synonymous. The conceptual differences between global and transnational media are rooted in their gatekeeping boundaries.

Transnational journalism can serve audiences on international and domestic levels. Therefore, local news can still serve domestic audiences but can also be shaped by an international outlook (Hellmueller, 2017, 8). Transnational journalism can be understood as the process of national news becoming global news—a transition still in progress.

Based on previous scholarship on global journalism, the following criteria can identify the concept:

Content: Global journalism features global issues (i.e., climate change; poverty; terrorism) as well as transnational issues (transnational effects of different people/events). Additionally, that content promotes non-parochial understandings and rejects ethnocentric/nationalist/partisan frameworks. Instead, the content includes diverse worldviews from global sources. Furthermore, the content is produced in multiple languages and includes important stories translated from foreign news networks. This approach could help cultivate a truly global audience (Berglez, 2013; Reese, 2010; Van Leuven and Berglez, 2016; Ward, 2005).

Institution: A global institution/network has bureaus worldwide, including headquarters outside of the West. Additionally, the network employs journalists from all over the world with an international education and multilingual skillset.

Ethics: Global journalism both in practice and in principle promotes content that serves citizens worldwide, offers voices from all over the world (not just one hemisphere), and features global consciousness, supporting the homogeneity of worldviews (Konieczna et al., 2014; Reese, 2010; Ward, 2005).

While scholarship focused exclusively on transnational journalism is limited, it should not be confused with global journalism. Therefore, I suggest that the following criteria can identify transnational journalism as:

Content: Features global issues (i.e., climate change, COVID-19, and terrorism) through a transnational lens (reports on how issues affect each country within their own cultural, geographical, and historical context). Additionally, news is not produced through a single global outlook but rather adopts different perspectives and sources in ways that best reflect the country being covered. This can get tricky because someone has to authorize this process in a manner that rejects ethnocentrism. However, journalists can avoid biased sourcing by broadcasting multiple voices from those directly affected by the issue or event.

Institution: Each news network works with outlets in other countries to represent the most accurate and ethical reporting. Due to the authoritarian nature of some nation states like China and Iran, transnational journalism allows for more nontraditional reporting and working with sources in different ways such as social media like Twitter, Facebook, and WhatsApp.

Ethics: This is where global and transnational journalism differ most. Transnational journalism adapts to different gatekeeping processes from multiple media systems and works within multiple codes of ethics rather than one universal code of ethics.

Transnational news media have been described as "deterritorialized," expanding knowledge beyond geographical limitations, educating Western viewers on international affairs, and bridging the gap between the Western audience and the "distant other in developing regions in the world" (Atad, 2017). CNN World and Al Jazeera are widely recognized as transnational news networks as they both have global access to sources worldwide, retain audiences that transcend national boundaries, and produce coverage of global level stories (i.e., stories that involve the majority of nations or the UN) that can be reported through a global lens as well as a national one (Hellmueller, 2017). Additionally, transnational journalists (or foreign correspondents) report from cities all over the world while serving their home audience and adapting "to the news-gathering principles of their foreign cities" (Hellmueller, 2017). On an organizational level, transnational journalism is an institution that develops a transnational agenda, such as pan-Arab or pan-European media, working around national boundaries (Hallin, 2009; Hellmueller, 2017).

One of the most important conceptual differences between global and transnational journalism is transnational journalism's ability to transcend national borders while maintaining domestic relevance (Hellmueller, 2017). Journalists at the local level are still able to choose their content, but they allow their stories to be shaped by a larger framework. In this way, domestic journalists are compelled to recognize the repercussions of their reporting. Given the shifting meanings that depend on cultural, political, and geographical contexts, it seems unnecessary to go beyond transnational journalism to form a global code of media ethics. If a global code of media ethics were constituted, inevitably, some key contexts would be overlooked or altogether negated in favor of postcolonial outlooks—a concept explored in more depth in the following section. Already Western viewpoints dominate the research around media studies in ethically questionable ways, particularly when observing Western news representations of women in the global South. Using women's social movements in the Middle East, this book aims to make a case for transnational journalism and transnational journalism ethics.

Chapter 2

Transnational Feminism and Alternative Media

Journalists are increasingly expected to do more with less while consistently keeping up with the news wires and publishing new content online. Inevitably, a lack of resources results in poor news quality. Journalists end up spending more time at their desks and less time engaging with sources, not to mention the very people they have been called on to serve. These challenges have provoked civilians around the world to cultivate alternative media spaces where their voices can be heard—including women from marginalized communities. By cultivating transnational feminist discourses on social and alternative media spaces, women from marginalized groups are responding to the effects of globalization by connecting with other women around the world.

Transnationalism is a term coined from the 1920s and "used to describe events and gatherings that bring people together across national borders" (Miller, 1999, 225) unofficially—meaning, not as representatives of any government body or organization. Similarly, transnational feminism illustrates the practice of working toward women's rights within shifting cultural, political, and geographical contexts (Fernandez, 2013)—crossing borders both literally and figuratively. Transnational feminism transcends the borders of nation states and adopts the idea that nationalism undermines feminism. Instead, transnational feminism underscores the intersectionality of women's oppression as they differ across multiple contexts, instead of working toward a fictitious "common good" dictated by the state.

Transnational feminism transpired partly in response to globalization—the broadening of social relations on a global scale (James, 2005). While historians date globalization processes to phenomena occurring centuries before the late 1900s, here I refer to the introduction of neoliberalism in the 1980s. Political and economic changes, as well as structural developments, transformed global flows of capital, where multinational organizations and corporations sought to enforce universal practices that were not necessarily representative of all affected parties (Kotz, 2002; Harvey, 2005).

As neoliberalism was entering Western society, newer forms of feminist politics emerged and addressed issues of difference and identity, including critiques from women of color concerning Western academic feminism. Some scholars refer to this period as "third-wave feminism,"—a feminist practice that "rejects grand narratives for a feminism that operates as a[n] hermeneutics of critique within a wide array of discursive locations, and replaces attempts at unity with a dynamic and welcoming politics of coalition" (Snyder, 2008, 176). Third-wave feminism is difficult to define but essentially embraces individual interpretations of feminism and multiple identities without engaging a specific agenda. In a way, third-wave feminism was a response to "second-wave" feminism—a movement distilled down to reflecting "antimale, antisex, antifemininity and antifun" (179). Moreover, third wavers proudly declare their multicultural and diverse identities while characterizing the second wave as a white, middle-class woman.

In contrast to this characterization of "second-wave" feminism, "third wavers" aimed to expand the feminist framework to be more inclusive and diverse, going as far as claiming the writings of feminists of color such as Gloria Anzaldúa, Cherríe Moraga, and Audre Lorde as the culmination of the third-wave movement (Snyder, 2008). However, these feminists of color, among others, played an important role in "second-wave" feminism and removing them falsely presents the "second wave [as] whiter than it was" (180). Some "second-wave" feminists responded to this cooptation by highlighting the third-wave movement as "whiter" than they recognized as many of the feminist experiences described by the third wave reflected "a white, middle-class bias" (181). Due to the problematic misconceptions within both the "second" and "third" waves, women activists and academics from the developing world saw this as an opportunity to contest "claims made on behalf of women, the conditions under which such claims were made, who makes the claims, for whom they are made, and whose interests are served by particular articulations of women's needs and interests" (Hawkesworth, 2006, 111). Thus, the practice of transnational feminism and the formation of transnational feminist networks were established.

The most important component of transnational feminism is that it rejects a single definition of feminism as well as the classic Western interpretations of feminism within scholarship and practice. Transnational feminism differs from international feminism because it defuses the overemphasis of a common "woman's experience" and instead recognizes the "inequalities across different groups of women" (Valoy, 2015), or what Kimberlé Williams Crenshaw (1990) refers to as intersectionality. In an effort to advance transnational feminist thought, scholars contributed to the literature on social movements and globalization by promoting a decolonized paradigm (Falcon, 2016). The decolonized paradigm shifts away from "dynamics that privilege English, liberalism, the global North, and so-called objectivist scientific modes of knowledge production" (p. 176) and instead cultivates a critical perspective of the elements that inform our research practices.

Transnational feminism intersects with journalism by challenging the "geopolitical eye"—a perspective that creates distance between international affairs and the audience. Instead, critical scholars and transnational feminists have adopted what is called the "anti-geopolitical eye"—"an eye that disturbs and disrupts the hegemonic foreign policy gaze" (O'Tuathail, 1996, 173). But scholars need not be the only ones to practice this disruption. By seeking out marginalized voices missing from mainstream media's hegemonic sphere, where neoliberalist ideology lives and breathes, journalists can practice their agency and engage the anti-geopolitical eye. Journalists can increase the proximity between "the observer and the observed" while asking tough questions that go beyond the surface—a sharp shift away from objectivity as this practice takes on a critical lens. The practice of objectivity in journalism has long been debated by both journalists and scholars, especially as it pertains to reporting on people of color. Objectivity privileges specific sources and certain information that helps maintain the status quo in society. I will expand on the problematic relationship between objectivity and journalism in more depth in chapter 8.

ALTERNATIVE-ACTIVIST NEW MEDIA

While mainstream journalists have been slow to embrace this critical work, practitioners of alternative-activist new media have been speaking truth to power for decades. Alternative-activist new media exists to alter society (Atton, 2002; Lievrouw, 2011). For the purpose of this book, alternative and/or activist media is defined as media that either employs or modifies "the communication artifacts, practices, and social arrangements of new information and communication technologies to challenge or alter dominant, expected, or accepted ways of doing society, culture, and politics" (Lievrouw, 2011, 19). Alternative-activist new media promotes three key components: (1) participation and interactivity; (2) time and space; and (3) diversity and horizontality (Fenton, 2016). *Participation and Interactivity*: This component "makes people active agents in the process of meaning-making" specifically by using new technology (Deuze, 2006, 66). In 2017, women in Iran launched #WhiteWednesdays on Facebook, Twitter, and Instagram. Women from Saudi Arabia, Afghanistan, and Turkey were encouraged to participate and interact with other women in this network. Women were able to form transnational solidarities with each other despite the geopolitical feuds taking place between their countries (i.e., Iran and Saudi Arabia). *Time and Space*: In 2014, activists in the West Bank reached out to protesters in Ferguson, Missouri, via Twitter with advice and words of encouragement as the two groups formed affective relationships with each other through the internet. Time and space were both superseded within these interactions due to globalized technology and transnational connections (Mislán and Shaban, 2018). *Diversity and Horizontality*: These components indicate that a hierarchy of leadership does not exist, nor is there is a screening process for who can or cannot protest (Tufekci and Wilson, 2012; Douai, 2013). In 2011, the Arab Spring erupted from Tunisia to Tahrir Square. Men and women protested alongside each other, and there was no screening process for who could or could not protest. People of all ages and ethnicities crowded the streets and the internet, sharing their lived experiences under authoritarian rule (Tufekci and Wilson, 2012; Douai, 2013).

Within transnational/global social movements, there are two ways activists can utilize media: (1) reconfiguration—users adapt existing technological tools to work for their needs and/or purposes; (2) remediation—users modify existing materials to encourage new ideas and networks of society (Lievrouw, 2011). This is evident in many transnational feminist movements in which the goal is to challenge "scattered hegemonies" (Grewal and Kaplan, 1994). Media can serve as a unique platform for women under authoritarian regimes where their voices and mobility are limited. For example, in Saudi Arabia, street protests are prohibited; however, state authorities practice leniency when it comes to social media campaigns. While digital protests are not beyond authoritarian control, these digital campaigns do challenge the authoritarian government's ability to censor online content—especially if it is not on an online publication or website (Zayani, 2015).

Furthermore, digital protest disrupts media monopolies and opens venues for alternative forms of engagement, particularly through social media (Hamdy, 2009); however, this does not make social media immune from being subsumed by those same media monopolies. But, to counteract "the growth of media power," activists form alternative media spaces and counter-publics (i.e., activist-run media platforms) (Mislán and Dache-Gerbino, 2018, 2624). Nevertheless, current activists are still more likely to utilize mainstream social media to benefit from the platforms' reach (Fuchs, 2015). Such is the case in Saudi Arabia where Saudis are among the world's top Twitter users (Zayani, 2018). On Twitter, Saudi women can negotiate their cultural restrictions by creating "alternative communities" where they can circumvent gender segregation and engage with Saudi men in a way not tolerated in public (p. 7). Within the sphere of autonomy, women can disseminate messages from the local space into the global space. Messages can also be domesticated—when a global movement becomes localized. For example, following the #MeToo movement's popularity, Mona Eltahawy, an Egyptian journalist and activist, tweeted her story of sexual assault in the holiest of sites in Islam—Mecca. Eltahawy encouraged other women to share their own harassment experiences during "hajj" (pilgrimage to Mecca) using the following: #MosqueMeToo. In one interview, Eltahawy mentioned that just because Muslim women's voices are not heard does not mean that they have nothing to say. Rather, they lack a platform from which to say it (Barron, 2018).

While movements like #MosqueMeToo may intentionally emerge from an influencer like Eltahawy, not all social movements go viral this way. For example: In December 2017, Viva Movahed stood on a utility box in downtown Tehran with a white scarf tied to the end of a stick to protest against Iran's compulsory hijab law. Someone took a photo of Movahed and posted it on social media, where eventually Movahed's image became the official symbol of the #WhiteWednesdays movement. Douai (2013) describes Movahed's role as "the accidental influential." The circulation of images like Movahed's can motivate people worldwide and mobilize transnational support that can pressure the authoritarian regime to cave. This is one method for cultivating counter-publics. The development of these counter-publics is crucial to the social movement's success as it serves as an alternative voice against the carefully structured narratives broadcasted from mainstream media. Furthermore, these counter-publics take on the issue of "gender visibility" in mainstream media by making women front and center (Hedge, 2011).

The #Daring2Drive campaign—a campaign aiming to eradicate the ban against women driving in Saudi Arabia—is another example of how Muslim women utilized both social and mainstream media to globally broadcast their narrative and pressure Saudi Arabia to eradicate the driving ban against women—a ban that was eventually lifted in September 2017 by Prince Mohammed bin Salman. Six years earlier, Manal al-Sharif (2017), one of the key women involved in the campaign, called on Saudi women to protest the ban by selecting a day to drive their cars in downtown Riyadh collectively. al-Sharif recognized the apprehension that came with defying the ban and decided to "test-drive" the act of protest to encourage Saudi women to participate. al-Sharif took the wheel while her friend and fellow activist filmed her driving and giving a monologue on the ban's absurdity. The video was later uploaded to YouTube and became an international sensation overnight with more than 700,000 views. The video led to al-Sharif's arrest but not merely because she was "driving while female," but more so because the authorities were threatened by the global attention she received on YouTube (al-Sharif, 2017).

TECHNOLOGICAL FETISHISM

While scholarship on new media and activism illustrates how technological tools can strengthen social movement campaigns, they can also hinder them. For example, in response to the #Women2Drive movement, counter-campaigns were created by anonymous users. Additionally, the Saudi government employed a "dumping policy" in which it "loaded hashtags of which it disapproves with many messages to divert attention from their main message," including #Daring2Drive (Maghlooth, 2013, 247). Authoritarian governments can also use social media to identify protesters by photo or online activity, as was the case in the 2009 Iran protests and throughout the Arab Spring (Lee et al. 2015; Thorsen and Sreedharan, 2019). Another threat to activist new media is the perpetuation of technological fetishism (Fuchs, 2012). Fetishizing technology can empower technologies with abilities they do not actually have (i.e., "the ability to solve social problems, to keep the economy vibrant, or to provide us with a superior life") (Harvey, 2003, 3; Comor and Compton, 2015). Furthermore, endowing technology with superficial powers can reduce societal issues "to the level of technology" (Fuchs, 2012, 286). Some news stories find the role of technology so alluring they make it the centerpiece of their story while simultaneously veiling the primary subject of the narrative—the women (Pennington and Birthisel, 2016). Perhaps Western media's focus on technology speaks to the "white savior" complex in which Arab revolutions are ushered into modernity by modeling their online activism after Western experiences with "internet revolutions" (Aouragh, 2012). However, just because "online activism *facilitates* offline liberation strategies" does not mean it contextualizes social movements within local politics (Aouragh, 2012, 529). In fact, online activism situates itself within global modernization.

The lack of contextualization is a symptom of the absence of voices from the ground. While social media can serve as a space for grassroots voices to be heard, to facilitate radical change, those voices must be acknowledged by those in power. Fenton (2015) said it best, "power must be wrested from those who have too much and reinvested in those who have too little" (p. 349). But how does one redistribute power when media platforms, understood to be spaces for radical ideas, are actually controlled by those who already maintain power? While some may argue for the power of alternative narratives, they are often spoken into the void as legacy media continues to dominate public discourse. Moreover, while social media introduces more sources for information, "mainstream news outlets still dominate our news consumption across all platforms with increasingly homogenous content" (Fenton, 2015, 354).

However, digital activists can leverage their own level of power through their privilege to access, both to technological tools as well as the powerful players whose attention they may capture. Radical change requires "democratically harnessing the dynamics of the international capitalist market to the needs and interests of the majority of citizens in any given political community" (Fenton, 2015, 353). But monetary capital need not be the only means of bargaining with the capitalist market. Digital activists can utilize their cultural capital to negotiate with those in power. By capitalizing on the public profile of a digital activist, social movements can access avenues of power and, subsequently, prompt "negotiation, compromise, reconciliation, bargaining, settlement, and occasionally, even consensus" (Fenton, 2015, 349).

But alternative-activist new media is not, and arguably should not be, the main outlet for news. However, by engaging with alternative-activist new media discourses, journalists can glean information on how to frame social movements accurately and the grassroots voices that make those movements possible.

REPRESENTING THE "OTHER" WOMAN

Transnational feminist scholars have argued that Western news representation of the "other," particularly Muslim women, is fabricated, exaggerated, or distorted to fit within the West's ideological framework (Mohanty, 1991; abu-Lughod, 2013; Farris, 2017). Given the geopolitical circumstances between the Western world (particularly the United States, the United Kingdom, and France) and the Middle East, media representations of women from these "other" countries are often laden with stereotypical narratives and ideological tropes of Muslims. Media ethics scholars argue that media maintain global power structures, including the construction of gender and sexuality—which can include popular frameworks for news stories featuring an oppressed/ repressed Muslim woman abused by Muslim men and their Islamic theology (Christians and Merrill, 2009).

With those constructions in mind, American journalists have practiced Orientalist framing of Muslim and Arab women (Said, 1989). News stories typically include narratives of Muslim women's oppression and repression from the men in their culture and religion. U.S. news outlets feature women in Middle Eastern and Muslim countries when their rights are disregarded, leading to a "confirmation bias" implying that Muslim women's rights are consistently violated because of their culture and religion. Furthermore, these narratives emphasize the need for Western liberation from their patriarchal societies (Mishra, 2007).

Edward Said (1978) developed the concept of Orientalism to describe the tense relationship between the "Oriental" and the "Occident," with the Occident displaying power over the Oriental. This ideology created an "us vs. them" framework that still exists today. In *Covering Islam*, Said (1980) focused on how the Middle East was portrayed by the West and unpacked how oriental depictions of the Middle East are reproduced through media, starting in the 1970s. These depictions are vital because, in the 1970s, Americans had little exposure to the Middle East and the region was predominantly featured in American news in relation to either oil, Iran, or terrorism.

Following the 9/11 attacks on the United States, American news media focused on two specific aspects of the Middle East—Islam and terrorism. While the 9/11 hijackers were self-proclaimed Muslims, news media unnecessarily used their Muslim identity to explain their terrorist practices, ultimately equating Islam with terrorism. However, not all Islamic countries were portrayed equally. While fifteen of the nineteen hijackers were from Saudi Arabia, with Osama bin Laden himself a former Saudi citizen, the country was portrayed as an ally in America's war on terrorism. Additionally, bin Laden's "right-hand man" was an experienced Egyptian terrorist; yet Egypt was also broadcasted as an ally. Separately, Iraq was framed as a threat to America and its values, though no Iraqis were involved in the attack (Ibrahim, 2009; Powell, 2011). The framing of these different countries could result from Saudi Arabia and Egypt's favorable relationship with the United States, both financially and geopolitically (Bagneid and Shneider, 1981; Herman 1993). Similar arguments have been made regarding President Trump's travel ban, commonly referred to as the "Muslim ban." Trump's executive order blocked nationals from seven Muslim majority nations from entering the United States for at least ninety days. These countries include Iraq, Syria, Iran, Libya, Somalia, Sudan, and Yemen. North Korea and Venezuela were also on the list. But rather than focus on which countries are on the list, it is important to notice who was not included—Egypt, Saudi Arabia, Turkey, and the United Arab Emirates (U.A.E). All four of these countries are in the same region and considered Muslim majority nations. The reasoning behind the ban was to protect the United States from terrorists; however, as previously noted, the majority of the 9/11 attackers were from Saudi Arabia. Two more were from the U.A.E., and one was from Egypt. However, none of the countries on the travel ban list include nationals with any history of terrorist activity against the United States. Some speculate that the reason these four countries are not on the list reflects their favorable business relationship with the United States, not to mention Trump himself (Gerstein and Lin, 2018; O'Brien, 2018; Giorgis, 2019).

While allies of the United States are often featured favorably in American news media, the same cannot be said of the countries' citizens. Women, specifically in Iran and Saudi Arabia, are victimized and portrayed as oppressed/repressed, docile bodies (Mishra, 2007; Seddighi and Tafakori, 2016). This is especially evident when focusing on women who wear hijab. In American media, hijab is often communicated as evidence of the Middle East's parochial ideology and backward practices (Said, 1980). That said, American media practice a sort of "confirmation bias" in which much of their news coverage features Arab and/or Muslim women in poor conditions, oppressive situations, and without a voice. However, what is not featured in the U.S. news media is hijab's historical context as an act of resistance and rebellion against American imperialism, as showcased during Iran's revolution (Hasan, 2018). By perpetuating Orientalist narratives surrounding women and hijab, transnational feminist efforts are negated in mainstream news media.

Western media outlets, particularly those in the United States, have long been criticized for their Orientalist framing of Muslim women (Said, 1989). These narratives typically emphasize Muslim women's oppression and the need for Western liberation from their patriarchal societies (Mishra, 2007). Historically, scholars have noted a connection between the media's framing of Muslim women as victims to "justify imperialism as a civilizing mission" (Farris, 2017, 76). While some of these narratives are worth considering, many still lack context—both cultural and political. In one study on American press coverage of Saudi women, Mishra (2007) found that not only did most of the articles lack context, they also omitted any examples of a Saudi woman's private life and focused exclusively on what could be observed in public.

In another study on the portrayal of Pakistani women in U.S. news, Rahman (2012) examined articles on Pakistani Muslim women in *Time* and *Newsweek* magazines from 1979 to 2002. The findings underscored the women as victims of Islam and blamed the religion for the women's struggles. Little coverage showcased Pakistani Muslim women as working toward freedom while practicing Islam but mostly featured them through a negative lens. One exception to the study includes the former prime minister of Pakistan, Benazir Bhutto. The prime minister was portrayed as a secular figure and was hardly ever associated with Islam. Bhutto's Western education at Oxford and Harvard was often highlighted, and, overall, she was portrayed in a positive light.

In Terman's (2017) study on the portrayal of Muslim women, she examined articles about women in non-U.S. countries published in the *New York Times* and *Washington Post*, within a thirty-five-year span—1980–2014. Results showed that the frequency of news coverage on Muslim women far outweighed those of non-Muslim women. These narratives predominantly focused on gender discrimination. These studies show that U.S. news

narratives tend to focus on stories about gender inequality in Muslim countries, even at the expense of a more substantial story. While gender inequality exists around the world, an uneven balance of coverage between women
in Muslim countries and women from other countries also exists (Terman,
2017). Within these news stories, Muslim women are routinely depicted as
poverty-stricken in war-torn countries, covered up and faceless, uneducated,
and ultimately passive victims in need of emancipation from the West. The
ways in which U.S. news coverage portrays Muslim women throughout the
world is important because many American audiences will not differentiate
between the portrayal of Muslims abroad and those who live in the United
States, which can deepen prejudices against Muslim communities.

Chapter 3

Activism, Feminism, and Women in Iran

Masih Alinejad is an exiled journalist from Iran and an activist currently living in Brooklyn, New York. In 2014, Alinejad started a Facebook page called "My Stealthy Freedom," where she invited women to join her in protesting against Iran's compulsory hijab law. The campaign evolved out of a photo Alinejad posted to her own page of her in a field without a hijab, expressing how free she felt. Iranian women resonated with Alinejad's photo and began sending her photos and videos of themselves also without hijab. Out of My Stealthy Freedom, White Wednesdays was born—a campaign peacefully protesting compulsory hijab law by women posting photos of themselves wearing white every Wednesday. Alinejad went on to publish a memoir about her life in Iran titled *The Wind in My Hair: My Fight for Freedom in Iran* in 2018. She's also been awarded the U.N. Watch's International Women's Rights Award, among other achievements (Human Rights Foundation, 2021). On the surface, Alinejad appears to be the ideal activist for women's rights in Iran; however, as Alinejad has started to gain influence in the Western world, her strategies may be shifting—for better or for worse. Following the 2017 Iranian protests against the regime, White Wednesdays made its way into the Western mainstream news cycle, requiring several interviews from Alinejad. Western media platforms allowed Alinejad to amplify the mission to eradicate compulsory hijab in Iran and provided her with opportunities to collaborate with Western leaders to make that mission a reality.

Alinejad was featured on several American news outlets from Fox News to NPR, criticizing Iran and calling for more sanctions on the country's leaders until they relent to Iranian women's demands. Alinejad's self-appointed role as spokesperson for Iranian women evolved into an issue of problematic representation following her meeting with U.S. Secretary of State Mike Pompeo. Alinejad met with Pompeo on February 4, 2019 (Palladino, 2019). At this

time, at least twenty-nine women in Iran were arrested for their involvement with White Wednesdays. According to Alinejad, she was invited to the
White House because she could speak to the events in Iran as someone "not
part of the power structure" and could see the need for change. She said,
"U.S. officials have realized that they can better understand the concerns of
a particular segment of Iran through me" (Rafat, 2019). Alinejad brought
three points of concern to Pompeo: (1) Iranians want an end to the Islamic
Republic; (2) The international community needs to hold Iran accountable
for forty years of human rights abuses; and (3) the Trump administration's
travel ban negatively affects the people, not the regime (Radio Farda, 2019).
However, Alinejad's relationship with the Trump administration would not
end with this meeting.

In 2019, Nick Muzin, a contentious Republican lobbyist, was awarded a
government contract to provide programming services for Voice of America
Persia—a U.S. government–supported media outlet focused on Iranian
affairs. Former journalists for VOA claim that since Muzin's take over, the
network became "a mouthpiece for Trump"—specifically advocating for
regime change in Iran. Before Muzin, right-wing groups, like The Heritage
Foundation (Dale, 2012), complained that VOA was not critical enough
of the Iranian regime and went as far as calling the network "pro-Iranian"
and "anti-American." The discourse would change with Muzin in charge.
Alinejad worked for VOA before Muzin's arrival. Since 2015, Alinejad has
served as the host for the 15-minute news segment, *Tablet*, featuring interviews with Iranian citizens. However, in 2020 Alinejad moved beyond her
post at VOA and was invited to speak on multiple news networks, including
CNN and Fox News, where she showed support for Trump's controversial
decision to assassinate Iranian Major General Qassim Soleimani. In each
of these segments, Alinejad was introduced as an independent journalist
and activist. Each network neglected to include Alinejad's position at VOA
(Fang, 2020). Additionally, there was no mention of Alinejad's contract
with the U.S. State Department, awarding her $230,000 for "her commen-
tary and anti-compulsory hijab activism in Iran" (Harvard, 2018). As soon
as this information went public, Alinejad faced judgment from the Iranian
community.

Alinejad's meeting with Pompeo received backlash from both women in
Iran and the diasporic Iranian community in the United States. Yet, the voices
of these women could not be found in mainstream news media. Alinejad later
clarified her role as a representative in an interview with Iran Wire: "I only
represent that part of the Iranian people who have trusted my media activities
in support of human rights in recent years. I do my best to represent these
people" (Shahrabi, 2019). Narratives like these become a breeding ground
for femonationalism and the perpetuation of Islamophobia in the name of

women's rights. However, the discourse was missing the voices of women involved in the movement on the ground in Iran. By neglecting to include these voices, mainstream Western media outlets were able to appropriate the women's social movements in Iran to promote their own political agendas, including regime change.

Narratives like Alinejad's helped to cultivate consent to go to war with Iran. In the same way that the voices of native informants like Ayaan Hirsi Ali and Azar Nafisi were used to justify the wars in Iraq and Afghanistan in the name of women's rights, Alinejad is the mouthpiece through which similar arguments are made. But where does the role of media play into this strategy? What responsibility do American journalists have in reporting multiple perspectives on women's experiences in Iran? Is it enough to broadcast Alinejad's recantations of her life in Iran? Does it simply fit with the Western feminist narrative that Muslim women want and need to be saved? To what extent was Alinejad's narrative weaponized? Respectable journalists like NPR's Terry Gross have interviewed Alinejad without challenging sweeping statements on the Iranian woman's experience. Why? Where are the voices of other women—specifically, women who disagree? Where is the exploration of the complexity of women's lives in Iran?

ACTIVISM AND WOMEN IN IRAN

Iranian women are no strangers to social movements. In fact, several Iranian women have been classified as leaders in both nationalist and anti-imperial campaigns. Iranian women's activism dates further back than 1979—back to the early nineteenth century when Tahereh Qurrat al-Ain (Fatemeh) became an influential leader of the Babi movement in 1848 and confronted the Qajar dynasty (1794–1925) by tearing off her veil and demanding emancipation for women. Fatemeh was eventually executed in 1852. But Iranian women were not deterred and continued to criticize the political and cultural environment within the state. For instance, in 1872, Naser al-Din Shah (1831–1896) organized "concessions and exclusive rights to British companies, in return for sums of money." Those concessions included "control over Persian roads, telegraphs, mills, factories, extraction of resources, and other public works" (Sahimi, 2010). At this time, Iran had a very lucrative tobacco crop. In 1890, Naser al-Din Shah gave Britain "a full monopoly over the production, sale, and export of tobacco for 50 years" in exchange for a sizeable sum and minimal profits and dividends. The Iranian people spoke back to this betrayal, and protests broke out in 1891, initiating the Tobacco Boycott, a movement largely made up of women protesting against foreign oppressors like Russia and Britain—including 300 women entering the Majlis (Iranian parliament) with pistols. In his book, *The Tobacco Boycott, The First Passive Resistance in Iran*, Ebrahim Taymouri describes women's involvement:

> Women's perseverance in this movement was such that when the ban on tobacco was announced, they led the protestors who were marching toward Naser al-din Shah palace. As they passed through the bazaar, the women closed down the shops.

One of these women included Zeynab Pasha, a leader in the Tobacco Boycott as well as other "rebellions against economic, injustices against merchants and peasants at the turn of the 20th century and later"—including the 1905 Constitutional Revolution. In 1934, she confronted Naser al-Din Shah once again after discovering that Iranian officials were hoarding flour to inflate bread prices—during a famine. Pasha did not merely march in the streets but led her fellow activists to force open doors of the wheat storehouses. Fair prices eventually returned (Zolqadr, 2020).

Pasha is just one example of many Iranian women involved in protests, including (1) the Constitutional Revolution (1905–1925), which fought for women's access to education and against polygamy and domestic violence; (2) the Era of Modern Nation Building (1920s–1940s), which included the expansion of women's programs and forced unveiling; (3) Nationalism (1940s–1960s), which showcased women's political activism through the cultivation of multiple women's political groups, granted women equal rights with men in terms of social insurance codes (maternity leave, benefits, disability); (4) Era of Modernization (1960s–1970s), which produced modern and professional working women, legal reforms like women's right to vote and changes to family law; however, many Iranian women believed these reforms to be superficial and distracting away from the lack of a free press, democratic elections, and increased censorship. Also during this time, only 26 percent of women in urban areas and 3 percent in rural areas were literate (Sahimi, 2010); (5) the Era of Islamist Revolution (1978–1997), which was built on an anti-imperialist, anti-monarchy messaging and included secular women protesting alongside Islamic women by veiling; (6) Post-Islamist Reform (1998–Present) which includes the "One Million Signatures" and the "Stop Stoning Forever" campaigns (2005–2006) as well as the current campaign to resist compulsory veiling laws (Tohidi, 2016).

The "Era of Modernization" is a key timeframe to focus on, largely because of the coup staged in 1953 by the CIA against Iran's elected prime minister Mohammed Mossadegh based on the leader's decision to nationalize the country's oil industry and deny any further Western involvement, specifically the British (Wu and Lanz, 2019). Iranian women marched in the streets alongside men in support of Mossadegh and against imperialism.

Nevertheless, the coup was successful, and the Shah—a strategic ally of the United States—was reinstated and ruled the country for another twenty-five years until the revolution in 1979. This intervention cultivated a distrust of Western governments and, consequently, a vilification of women's movements as a "feminist deviation under the western influence" and accusing activists of "being agents in a U.S. plan for regime change" (Tohidi, 2010, 406). Interestingly, this "cultural penetration" did not apply to men. The revolution in 1979 saw that "[women's rights] were overtly violated in the name of indigenous culture, self-reliance, individual emancipation and an end to all forms of domination of one human being or a country over another" (Sreberny and Khiabany, 2010, 93). Discursively, women are the personified versions of their nation state, which allows for the understanding that the policing of women is parallel to the safeguarding of the nation. The veil became an overarching narrative for that policing.

One of the most memorable remnants of the 1979 revolution was Ayatollah Khomeini's forced veiling of Iranian women. Western feminists rose up in protest against this new law that went beyond a call for modest clothing. As Betty Friedan, author of *The Feminine Mystique*, noted in a *New York Times* article, "the veil symbolized status for women under traditional Islam that denied them rights to their children in the event of divorce, made them vulnerable to easy divorce and to the possibility of polygamous marriage" (Cummings, 1979, para. 9). Western feminists saw Iranian women's resistance to the veil as an opportunity to pursue an international movement with women from New York, Paris, London, and Rome. Specifically, renowned American feminists like Gloria Steinem, Robin Morgan, and Betty Friedan organized a demonstration in front of the Rockefeller Center in New York City, where the office of representatives of Iran's provisional government is located. At this same time, another prominent American feminist, Kate Millet, was actually in Iran marching in women's rights demonstrations and also attempting to speak at an event on International Women's Day—a conference in support of Iranian women—though it is not clear that Iranian feminists invited her to speak at all. In fact, Millet was originally invited to the country by an Iranian man she worked with previously. Following Millet's experience and eventual expulsion from Iran, Millet became aware of the difference between Iranian women's protest and those of Western feminists—"it is impossible to equate the experience of Western sisters who demonstrate for several hours outside the Rockefeller Center in New York with those of Iranian women who risk their lives when they march in the streets as feminists" (Naghibi, 2007, 98). While these feminists may have been well-intentioned in attempting to form a "global sisterhood," Nima Naghibi (2007) argues that "by turning Iranian feminist concerns into an international women's concern, the particularity and specificity of anti-imperialist Iranian feminism was elided" (p. 100).

Naghibi's argument suggests that Iranian women cannot fight for both gender equality and anti-imperialism.

Islamic clerics were able to use this Western appropriation to defuse the anti-imperialist Iranian feminist movement by arguing that feminism was indeed a "Western phenomenon" and therefore, "counter-revolutionary behavior," perpetuating a distorted binary between the West and Iran (p. 101). Since then, suspicions of any relationship with Western entities have damaged the potential for the establishment of transnational feminist networks, preventing women like the 2003 Nobel Peace Prize winner Shirin Ebadi from accepting grants from international donors for fear of being considered a threat to Iran's national security. Thus, while Iranian women activists are caught between "Islamic masculine forces inside Iran" and "secular hegemonic forces in the West," they are making democratic efforts to separate themselves from both patriarchal societies (Tohidi, 2010, 407). However, this begs the question of whether or not Western feminists are exempt from supporting Iranian women's protest or any woman's protest outside of the Western world. Arguments like Naghibi's create a problematic framework implying that Iranian women can either work toward gender equality or anti-imperialism. The framework completely ignores the intersectionality that makes up the Muslim woman. Similarly, Black women in the United States have faced the problematic binary between gender equity and racial equity (Wingfield, 2020). The discrimination and problematic media framing Muslim women face are not only because they are women or only because they are Muslim. Their intersectionality is what makes their experience unique.

In *Notes Towards A Performative Theory of Assembly*, Judith Butler argues against this dialectic of gender equality versus anti-imperialist causes. Western feminists are not bound to imperialist ideologies. But if Western feminists were to become detached from women's campaigns throughout the world, their solidarity would be rooted in proximity and sameness. Moreover, there are times when it is necessary for Western feminists to recognize women's struggles in different contexts on a global level. Butler (2018) argues to this point:

> The body cannot be relieved of its locatedness, its exposure, through its mediated transport. In one sense, the event is emphatically local, since it is precisely the people there whose bodies are at risk. But if those bodies on the line are not registered elsewhere, there is no global response, and also no global form of ethical recognition and connection, and so something of the reality of the event is lost. It's not just that one discrete population views another through certain media moments but that such a response makes evident a form of global

connectedness, however provisional, with those whose lives and actions are registered in this way. (105)

Those mediated moments exchanged between women on a global scale have taken to the internet in a way that is transforming the reach of transnational feminism—where the distance between "here" and "there" can be transcended.

IRANIAN WOMEN IN CYBERSPACE

Within the post-Islamic reform era (1998–present), Iranian women have taken to the internet to cultivate a public space dedicated to women, particularly the blogosphere. Blogs became a space where Iranian women could showcase the personal as political, naming "socially and culturally sensitive issues" and making them "political concerns" (Sreberny and Khiabany, 2010, 113). Furthermore, Iranian women also utilized social media platforms like Facebook and Twitter to circumvent state control of public spaces like mainstream media and on-the-ground campaigns. In interviews with Iranian women feminists and activists, Gheytanchi and Moghadam (2014) found that activists believed "their encounter with social and women's rights issues within cyberspace provided them with a safe environment to explore new venues and express their feelings of frustration with the status quo" (p. 9). Social media also equipped the Egyptian "Facebook Girl" Israa Abdel Rattah "to organize a campaign of civil disobedience to protest the deteriorating conditions of the average citizen," reminiscent of Zeynab Pasha's own activism (p. 12). One of the most notable movements led by Iranian women activists was the 2006 One Million Signatures Campaign (OMSC). The purpose of the campaign was to promote the evolution of women's rights in Iran, including "support of changes to discriminatory laws against women" (Change for Equality, 2006). Activists worked to collect the signatures primarily through door-to-door contact but also via meetings and the internet. The OMSC evolved into "a loose, informal transnational network" with a chapter in California, continuing to reflect "the entire campaign's desire to be horizontal and grassroots, rather than hierarchical and bureaucratic" (Sameh, 2010, 448). In 2008, OMSC grabbed the attention of Amnesty International and, consequently, the world (Sreberny and Khiabany, 2010). For these activists, the internet facilitated both "connectivity and mobilisation to an unprecedented level" which contributed to a "feminization of the public sphere" (Moghadam and Sadiqi, 2006). But, while these platforms are advantageous for Iranian women's movements, these online initiatives are not limited to campaigning.

What makes Iranian women's utilization of the internet different from other online projects is the link between activism and nuanced discourse (Sreberny and Khiabany, 2010). This bridge evolved into a transnational network of women's shared experiences within the MENA region. These loose networks have been strengthened by relationships with Satellite TV channels like *al-Jazeera, al Arabia, CNN International,* and the *BBC* to help "counter the state's monopoly over the news" (Gheytanchi and Moghadam, 2014, 7). Additionally, Iranian women used alternative media sites like Maydaan and IranDokht.com to connect Iranian women with the global sphere (Sreberny and Khiabany, 2010), thus forming transnational connections with women all over the world and setting the stage for the next big women's movement. That movement was White Wednesdays.

In late 2017, protests in Iran erupted against the government due to the government's dramatic increase in oil prices resulting from U.S. sanctions on Iranian oil exports. Within those larger protests was a different campaign, unassociated with the widely circulated government protests. Viva Movahed stood on a utility box in downtown Tehran to protest against the country's compulsory hijab law. Movahed's image was circulated via social media, and she became the unofficial symbol of the movement #WhiteWednesdays. #WhiteWednesdays is an online campaign featuring women from Iran, Saudi Arabia, Afghanistan, and others posting photos and videos of themselves either wearing a white scarf or nothing on their heads at all to show solidarity with other women protesting against compulsory hijab (Alinejad, 2018). While women in neighboring countries showed support, there was a questionable silence from Western feminists, most notably from women like Linda Sarsour, organizers of the women's march, and the Swedish prime minister who wore a hijab on her most recent visit to Iran. There was some speculation that the absence of a response from Western feminists was rooted in their loyalty to Obama's decision to join the Nuclear Deal with Iran—especially since the deal was predominantly negotiated by women, including U.S. Undersecretary of Political Affairs, Wendy Sherman (Kianpour, 2015). Additionally, some journalists suggested that Western feminists, like Linda Sarsour, did not want to appear Islamophobic, particularly while working to normalize hijab in their own countries—consequently making up for their false pretenses for supporting Muslim women in the past.

Right-wing, conservative journalists took advantage of this silence and began to control the Western narrative surrounding #WhiteWednesdays, almost, if not, by default. These journalists began to criticize Western feminists by highlighting the bravery of women in Iran who risk imprisonment or death by publicly removing their hijabs. Furthermore, self-described Trump supporters and right-wing nationalists from the United States the United Kingdom, and Canada began to cultivate a femonationalist discourse on Twitter. Femonationalism is a term created by Sara Farris (2017) that describes rhetoric utilizing feminist and gender-equality language to promote anti-Islamic and xenophobic campaigns, usually practiced by right-wing, conservative Westerners. For example, some right-wing, conservative journalists used their platforms to weaponize Iranian women who are flogged for "bad hijab" to demonize hijabi women in the United States, like Linda Sarsour, who claims hijab as a form of freedom (Hasan, 2018). This discourse assumes a singular definition of hijab and what it stands for while neglecting the transnational context of hijab.

WHY DOES WESTERN MEDIA KEEP GETTING IT WRONG?

Western media outlets have long been infatuated with Muslim women, using Orientalist tropes to illustrate their plight in a world described as an archaic, Islamic dictatorship of oppression and repression. More recently, a neo-orientalist approach has been found within Western media discourse and feminist scholarship on Arab women, particularly their role in the Arab Spring. Arab feminist scholars had expressed frustration regarding these Western narratives and responded with historical accounts of Arab women's activism that date far before the Arab Spring and engaged in movements beyond women's rights (Abu-Lughod and El-Mahdi, 2011; Gheytanchi and Moghadam, 2014). Abu-Lughod (2013) speaks to this issue at length in her well-known book *Do Muslim Women Need Saving?* The introduction brings the reader into a conversation between Abu-Lughod and an Egyptian woman named Zaynab. Abu-Lughod explains to Zaynab why she is writing this book and "how people in the West believe that Muslim women are oppressed." Zaynab expressed that Muslim women are indeed oppressed but not by Islam. She says, "The government oppresses women. The government doesn't care that they don't have work or jobs, that prices are so high that no one can afford anything. Poverty is hard. Men suffer from this too" (1). This conversation took place just three weeks before the Tahrir Square protests in 2011.

U.S. news media have perpetuated misconceptions about Middle Eastern women that have circulated stereotypical tropes of Arab and Muslim women across the Western world. However, with the introduction of the Arab Spring, Westerners became more aware of Arab women's involvement in human rights issues and social movements, though women's activism was present long before 2011. Several prominent Arab women scholars and activists have spoken out against the misconception that Arab and Muslim women began protesting against injustice with the emergence of the Arab Spring (Mohanty, 1991; Keddi, 2007; Abu-Lughod and El-Mahdi, 2011; Holt and Jawad,

2013). Rabab El-Mahdi (2011), a scholar and activist, finds this impression to be "deeply troubling on a number of levels." She says:

> It assumes that women were somehow dormant or passive—we want to know how they suddenly became active in the revolution. It dismisses the role that female workers have played in the wave of labor mobilization since 2006, the role of female activists in the prodemocracy and antiwar movements since 2003, and their constant presence in the student movement, just to name a few.

Historically, Arab and Muslim women's activism was mostly aligned with nationalist and anti-colonial movements, going back to the Ottoman Empire when British and French imperialists took over the Middle East. Many women were involved in the Egyptian revolution in 1919, including organizing militant nationalist demonstrations. Around this same time, Iraqi and Palestinian women also fought alongside men in their anti-colonial endeavors. In the 1950s and 1960s, Algerian women were heavily involved in the Battle of Algiers as nurses, fighters, bomb planters, message carriers, and weapon smugglers. Even before 1979, women in Iran participated in demonstrations with communist and socialist parties. In 1922, Iranian women cultivated the "Patriotic Women's League of Iran" in response to the lack of gender reform following the Constitutional revolution. Additionally, Kuwaiti women in the 1990s fought for their right to vote and stand for election (Keddi, 2007). Women from all over the Arab world and beyond have participated, led, and initiated steps toward liberation, defying Western stereotypes as passive victims.

Some of the feminist movements carried out by Arab and Muslim women included calls that depart from the traditional, Western understanding of feminism. For example, Egyptian women launched a domesticity movement which "encouraged women to be educated, mainly in order to bring up educated sons, to adopt more healthful practices in homemaking and child rearing, and to take on new responsibilities" that would cultivate a more "autonomous nuclear family" (Keddie, 2007, 91). Additionally, in the 1930s, women in Syria and Lebanon encouraged "patriotic motherhood" as they served as allies to the nationalist movement.

However, for all the efforts those women have put forth, women are still undervalued, underrepresented, and exploited by mainstream news media. This has led many women to embrace an Islamist approach (not to be confused with an Islamic approach), using the framework of Islam to generate support for women's rights. Muslim women have recognized that "some men use Islam to violate women's rights because of their lack of knowledge about the religion rather than the religion itself" (Holt and Jawad, 2013, 61).

This approach is known as "Islamist feminism," in which Muslim women use the discourse of Islam to bring liberation to women without the threat of Western hegemony. This discourse encourages modernization without Westernization. Many women have felt empowered by Islamic activism, and while not all reformist movements are specifically "Islamic," women have used the Islamic framework as a form of resistance, challenging male-dominated interpretations of the Qur'an while also working not to be categorized with Western notions of feminism. The debate surrounding feminism in Arab-Muslim society "is not easy to detach [from] the Arab world's experiences of European colonialism from notions of natural or indigenous development" (Holt and Jawad, 2013, 62). In fact, even when government institutions recognize women's rights, "tribal customs still dominate," which could partially explain women's fervent involvement in the Arab Spring—specifically Egypt and Yemen where women believe that despite their efforts in previous revolutions, their lives have only become worse, not just for women but for their people as a whole.

Since the 9/11 attacks, the world consistently consumes victimizing narratives of Muslim women needing to be rescued from their Islamic culture. Americans all over the political spectrum are quick to call out patriarchy when it is taking place somewhere else. As Abu-Lughod (2013) argues, "Muslim women's issues regularly stir up international debate in ways that concerns about women elsewhere in the world do not" (14). By shifting the gaze from domestic to global women's issues, mainstream news media ignored the oppressive practices against women in the United States and instead mobilized around problematic "cultural" issues like "female genital cutting, enforced veiling, or the honor crime" within the American humanitarianism framework (Abu-Lughod, 2012, 8). While the world consistently keeps a watchful eye on Muslim women, many women's issues within the Western world are overlooked. The obsession with Muslim women and the veil reigns supreme and politicizes Islam in problematic ways. However, transnational feminism recognizes "the dangers of appropriation by a new imperialist agenda" (Siddiqi, 2011, 183). Siddiqi (2011) asks an important question about representation and living in the modern world:

> What, if any, are the implications of the representational politics and practices of human rights activists who are local but who operate within circuits of transnational modernity? (183)

This book uses the White Wednesdays campaign in Iran to explore similar questions featured in the following chapters.

Chapter 4

Native Informants and Femonationalism

The attacks on September 11 solidified the stereotypical tropes used against Muslim men and women—the man as a barbaric misogynist and the woman a docile victim—and created the transnational "war on terror" narrative that perpetuates Islamophobia and supports neoliberal economic agendas. Since 2013, countries like the Netherlands, France, and Italy have elected right-wing leaders who have capitalized on this narrative, specifically by stigmatizing Muslim men in a supposed effort to support Muslim women. This negative connotation has aided right-wing parties in making their rhetoric acceptable to the mainstream and, consequently, gaining support in elections (Farris, 2017). Ironically, the very parties that verbally launched a crusade for Muslim women's rights conveniently overlooked their own sexist practices— avoiding issues of the gender pay gap or women's roles in policymaking. Nevertheless, heads of state like France's Marine Le Pen called for national security advocates, claiming that immigrants are attacking the country's secular culture—particularly Muslims "who introduced communitarianism into French society and thus threaten not only a pillar of the republic, but also the unity of the nation" (Farris, 2017, 34). According to Le Pen and past French leaders, the presence of veiled women demonstrates the attack on the country's secular culture. Le Pen's ideology is reminiscent of Suad Joseph's (1999) argument that while the state consists of its individual citizens, it is women who "become prime actors in the construction of new cultural forms" (p. 180)—meaning, the image of women in society reflects the culture of that society. However, while the figure of the woman represents a nation, the ideological sexism rooted in the nation state constrains her rights as a citizen of that nation (Alarcón, Kaplan, and Moallem, 1999). A woman's voice is only amplified when it assimilates to the state's agenda, and with the help of mainstream media, that narrative can go a long way.

Mainstream media have a long history of perpetuating ideological positions that benefit the state's agenda (Riker, 1986). The relationship between media and the state was particularly evident throughout the conception and execution of the "war on terror" and the American invasion of both Afghanistan and Iraq. Following the 9/11 attacks, the Bush administration's national policy launched the "war on terror" narrative that was widely accepted across the political spectrum (Entman, 2003). American journalists quickly latched on to this rhythmic policy phrase, internalized its ideology within their reporting, and, essentially, helped brand the phrase as public opinion (Reese and Lewis, 2009). The "war on terror" evolved into a framing device that helped the media interpret and justify the United States' invasion of Afghanistan and Iraq.

Specifically, throughout the Bush, Obama, and Trump administrations, the "War on Terror" emphasized the responsibility for American troops to protect the women and children within Afghanistan. Prior to 9/11, Afghan women were rarely covered in U.S. news; however, following the attacks, mainstream news media consistently highlighted the oppression of Afghan women, particularly their forced veiling as a human rights violation. The narrative perpetuated by U.S. media helped garner public support for the war in Afghanistan by utilizing a rallying cry to liberate Afghan women. Furthermore, throughout the Obama and Trump administrations, the narrative evolved into a need for American troops to remain in Afghanistan to ensure the maintenance of the liberties gained by women there over the years (Hafez and Luqiu, 2020). However, the Trump administration eventually worked toward securing a peace deal with the Taliban and removing American troops from the country while women's rights remained at risk. As Hafez and Luqui (2020) argue, "the U.S. abandoning this mission further supports our points that Afghan women have simply served as ideological justification for U.S. interests" in Afghanistan, "one reinforced by media year after year" (14). Similar arguments were made that the Bush administration justified the occupation in Iraq in the name of women's rights (Al-Ali and Pratt, 2009).

Though it is important to note that white Western leaders do not always make for an effective campaign on their own; however, "native informants" can help propagate imperialist agendas in stealthy ways. Native informants are those "voluntarily contributing to colonial and Islamophobic discourses by presenting their narratives as archetypes and representatives of 'traditions' or 'cultures'" (Rahbari, 2020, 3). Native informants' consistent collaboration with American media perpetuates harmful and damaging narratives on a grand scale and circulates the ongoing fear of Muslim men that attempts to control Muslim women both in the West and in their home countries. Feminists such as Ayaan Hirsi Ali, a Somali-born Dutch American writer, and Azar Nafisi, the Iranian American author of *Reading Lolita in Tehran*, have been characterized as native informants by weaponizing their experiences to highlight women's rights issues within the Muslim world. While no one denies their encounters with injustice, Hirsi Ali and Nafisi both nullify the experiences of Muslim women that do not mirror their own. Understandably, both women left their home countries at a young age and found refuge within the Western world, where they lead successful careers. In 1969, Hirsi Ali was born in Somalia and forced to undergo female genital mutilation (FGM) at a young age. In 1992, Hirsi Ali's father planned to force her to marry a distant cousin. To escape this fate, she fled to Holland and claimed political asylum and, eventually became a citizen. She has since dedicated her life to raising awareness of women's rights issues, including honor killings and FGM. Her career has included a position in the Dutch parliament from 2003 until 2006. During this time, she created a short film about Islam's oppression of women and was named one of *Time* magazine's "100 Most Influential People" in 2005. In 2006, the Dutch courts attempted to revoke Hirsi Ali's citizenship based on misunderstandings regarding her asylum. She eventually moved to the United States, where she founded the AHA Foundation—a nonprofit that works to protect Muslim women from violence. She is also the author of the *New York Times'* best-selling book, *Infidel* and *The Caged Virgin: An Emancipation Proclamation for Women and Islam* (AHA Foundation, 2021; Hoover Institute, 2021). Both books perpetuate narratives that negate Muslim women's agency and demonize Muslim men.

In the 1970s, Azar Nafisi traveled to the United States to pursue higher education and eventually earned a PhD from the University of Oklahoma. Nafisi returned to Iran in 1981 to teach at the University of Tehran (where her best-selling book is based). She was discharged from her position after refusing to wear the mandatory veil and did not return to teaching until 1987 at the Free Islamic University and Allameh Tabatabai University in Iran. Nafisi eventually left Iran in 1997 and made her home in the United States where she served as a Fellow at the Foreign Policy Institute of Johns Hopkins University's School of Advanced International Studies until 2017. Nafisi published *Reading Lolita in Tehran* in 2003, shortly before the Iraq war. The book has been translated into 32 languages and spent more than 117 weeks on *The New York Times'* bestseller list. The problematic nature of the book is its limited perspective on Iran and unending praise of Western culture, particularly Western literature. Nafisi has gone on to write for *The New York Times*, *Washington Post*, and *The Wall Street Journal*. Additionally, her cover story, "The Veiled Threat: The Iranian Revolution's Woman Problem," was published in *The New Republic* in 1999 and reprinted in several languages (Fresh Air, 2003; AzarNafisi.com, 2021). Interestingly, it is important to note that these highly esteemed media outlets that have long denied space for Muslim women's voices transform into a platform for former Muslim women's voices with narratives that assimilate to the state's agenda—the war on terror.

Hirsi Ali and Nafisi both illustrate success stories coming out of the presumably violent Muslim world; however, they have both allowed their lived experiences to be weaponized to maintain Islamophobic and anti-immigrant policies—hence their characterization as native informants. Native informants tend to be born in places within the Middle East or Muslim majority countries and eventually migrate to Europe or the United States to pursue higher education. Additionally, there is a tendency for the informant to feel disconnected from their culture of origin, but that does not necessarily imply their belongingness to the Western country where they now reside. Instead, they find an outlet to use their anthropological knowledge of the homeland as a way to establish a successful career. Hamid Dabashi (2011) compares native informants to "Harriet Beecher Stowe's Uncle Tom and Malcolm X's House Negro" (15). Like Uncle Tom and the House Negro, the native informant's ability to freely criticize their cultures is only "made possible by the protection they enjoy when they relocate to the centers of Western European and North American power" (17). They not only internalize orientalist tropes of their home societies but become experts in perpetuating those harmful stereotypes.

Edward Said (2003) addressed the danger underneath the manipulating narratives wielded by native informants promoting Orientalism and Islamophobia. Said (2003) specifically refers to the invasion of Iraq in 2003, citing the influential rhetoric of Bernard Lewis and Fouad Ajami—in fact, the term "native informant" was first used in reference to Ajami in an article for *The Nation* by Adam Shatz (2003). Lewis, a British historian, and Princeton professor, exerted incredible influence over the Bush administration's foreign policy with the Middle East—particularly Iraq. Lewis argued that acts of terrorism like those of 9/11 were a result of the deteriorating Islamic civilization working to preserve religious fundamentalism. The solution, Lewis claimed, was to bring democracy to Iraq because "Either we bring them freedom, or they destroy us." Lewis wrote articles for *The Wall Street Journal*, *The New Yorker*, and *The Atlantic*—including a cover article in 1990 titled, "The Roots of Muslim Rage." Additionally, he wrote a best-selling book discussing the lead-up to the 9/11 attacks, *What Went Wrong? The Clash Between Islam and Modernity in the Middle East*. He was also featured in interviews with NBC's "Meet the Press" (the evening before the start of the Iraq war) and PBS with Charlie Rose (Martin, 2018).

Fouad Ajami, a Lebanese Shia Muslim with an Iranian family, started his career as a pro-Palestinian commentator up until the 1980s (Hamidaddin, 2014; Kechichian, 2014). Ajami immigrated to the United States as an Arab nationalist in 1963, four years before the 1967 war in Lebanon, and attended

Eastern Oregon College before earning a doctorate at the University of Washington. In 1980, Ajami began teaching at Johns Hopkins, where he began to adopt an Islamophobic rhetoric and joined a right-wing Zionist group. Ajami quickly became an esteemed American political scientist and is said to have been "the most politically influential Arab of his generation" (Martin, 2014). American news networks often featured him as an expert in Middle Eastern affairs, including CBS News, CNN, and PBS's "Charlie Rose and "News Hour" (Martin, 2014). He also advised American policymakers and, like Lewis, Ajami was also a proponent for the war in Iraq (in 1991 and 2003), believing that democracy could solve the issues in the Middle East. He claimed, "Arabs are to blame for everything and therefore deserve 'our' contempt and hostility" (Said, 2003). Said argues for the imperativeness of recognizing the presence of these native informants and their influence not only on American policymakers but also on the American people via mainstream news. These narratives highlight Islam as the antithesis to secularization and modernization, which not only affects the American perspective of Muslims abroad but also those living within the United States. These narratives encourage assimilation and wariness of anyone who deviates from Western norms, no doubt a product of Western thought's binary nature.

While native informants are often associated with right-wing politicians and Islamophobes, it is important to note that native informants do not necessarily need to align with right-wing politicians to benefit their agendas. For example, Mona Eltahawy, an Egyptian journalist and activist residing in New York City, is very much a liberal feminist and a critic of the patriarchy, not to mention the Trump administration. Yet her words, both in columns and books, support the Islamophobic rhetoric coming out of the very same administration. Eltahawy's (2012) article "Why Do They Hate Us?" was featured in *Foreign Policy* magazine and served as the cover for that issue. The article comes on the heels of the Arab Spring in 2011. Eltahawy was assaulted during the protests in Tahrir Square and her words sharing her lived experience as both an Egyptian and Muslim woman are noteworthy. However, her sweeping remarks associating all Arab countries as hating women are not. Eltahawy's article places a large emphasis on Arab and Muslim women and sex—specifically citing the virginity tests and sexual harassment against women in Egypt. Eltahawy later published a book in 2015 titled *Headscarves and Hymens: Why the Middle East Needs a Sexual Revolution*. Several of the same arguments in the *Foreign Policy* article overlap with the book's content. Like Hirsi Ali and Nafisi, Eltahawy has been able to capitalize on her lived experience by publishing rhetoric that ignores the complex reality of the Muslim world. Instead, she produces the material necessary to solidify the confirmation biases the West holds for Muslim women. Academic scholars such as Lila Abu-Lughod, Leila Ahmed, and Saba Mahmood argue against the notions presented by native informants. They highlight these testimonies as justification for imperialism, as was the case in Afghanistan when George W. Bush claimed that the war on terror would help liberate Afghan women (Marks, 2012). The Islamophobic rhetoric from native informants wrongfully conflates all Muslim women's experiences. The blanket statements made about Muslim women echo those made by Western feminists for decades, using the West's concept of liberation as the evaluation of success in women's movements.

Native informants can take on various forms, especially when it comes to women's rights in the Muslim world. Masih Alinejad could, arguably, be considered a native informant. While she first found her voice on American airwaves telling her own story of oppression in Iran, she quickly rose to the level of an "unofficial" foreign policy expert—specifically regarding the 2017 national protests against the Islamic Republic as well as the assassination of Qassem Soleimani in January 2020. Major Iranian General Qassem Soleimani was killed on January 3, 2020, after President Trump ordered a drone strike near the Baghdad airport. The geopolitical relationship between Iran and the United States had been tense since the Trump administration pulled out of the Nuclear Deal with Iran in 2018 and continued to grow worse throughout the tenure of the Trump presidency. However, after an Iranian-backed militia attacked a U.S. military base in northern Iraq, killing an American defense contractor, Nawres Hamid, and injuring several coalition troops, Trump ordered a missile strike against the militia. This resulted in a retaliatory response on the U.S. Embassy in Baghdad and ended with a drone strike from the United States that killed Soleimani (Davis, 2020; Salim et al., 2020).

Following Soleimani's death, Iranian news outlets broadcast footage of hundreds of thousands of Iranians gathering to mourn. However, Alinejad claimed that this footage was nothing more than Iranian propaganda. Alinejad was repeatedly featured on Fox News to provide commentary on the Iranian people's reaction to the leader's assassination, specifically using one headline reading, "Inside Perspective on How the Iranian People Viewed General Soleimani." Alinejad used the platform to speak for "the average Iranian citizen" and "the Iranian people" while leveraging her popularity on social media to vouch for her credibility to make such claims:

> I have more than 4 million followers on various social media networks, and I have received thousands of messages, voice mails and videos from Iranians in cities such as Shiraz, Isfahan, Tehran and even Ahvaz, who are happy about Soleimani's death…there are many Iranian voices who think Soleimani was a war criminal, but Western journalists rarely reach out to them. (Musto, 2020)

While Alinejad may very well have received such messages, there's no proof outside of her multiple interviews with Martha MacCallum. Granted, messages of dissent could be suppressed because of the Iranian regime's no-tolerance policy for such discourse; however, quotes from one exiled journalist are not enough. Alinejad's role here is reminiscent of Dabashi's (2011) critique of *Reading Lolita in Tehran* author Azar Nafisi, a native informant who "speaks for the white-identified, transnational bourgeoisie that calls her 'the voice of the modern Iranian woman'" (28). The voice of this modern Iranian woman is imperative to the justification of Western intervention, especially when concerning women's rights in the Muslim world.

It is also worth noting the Iranian and Iranian American voices that were scarcely present in the narrative surrounding American news coverage of White Wednesdays. Azadeh Moaveni is an Iranian American journalist, writer, and academic who has written on the Middle East for highly esteemed U.S. publications such as *Time* magazine, *The New York Times*, and *The New Yorker*. In 2018, Moaveni wrote a piece for *The New Yorker* titled, "How the Trump Administration is Exploiting Iran's Burgeoning Feminist Movement" that unpacks how former secretary of state Mike Pompeo weaponized the White Wednesdays movements to "isolate the Islamic Republic and promote regime change in Iran" (para. 3). The article goes into depth on how the Trump administration's withdrawal from the Nuclear Deal has actually undermined the women's movement by creating economically unstable conditions for all Iranians. The article includes a statement from Sussan Tahmasebi, the director of FEMENA—an organization that supports women's rights defenders throughout the MENA and Asia regions. Tahmasebi is also an Iranian woman and one of the founding members of the Iranian women's movement, including the One Million Signatures Campaign in 2006. Outside of Tahmasebi's feature on NPR and Movaeni's article in *The New Yorker*, their voices were essentially absent from the U.S. mainstream news cycle, even though they offered a more nuanced narrative than the one circulated by Alinejad. Moreover, both women have excellent credentials that should have privileged them as star sources; yet they were underutilized. Their discourse did not concur with the state agenda.

FEMONATIONALISM

Sara Farris (2017) introduced the theoretical concept of "femonationalism"—a utilization of feminism and gender-equality language to promote anti-Islamic and xenophobic campaigns, usually practiced by right-wing, conservative Westerners. Femonationalist discourse thrives on orientalist tropes that depict

Arab and Muslim women as victims of Muslim men and, subsequently, Islam (Seddighi and Tafakori, 2016; Farris, 2017). Femonationalism is typically practiced by four groups: (1) right-wing nationalists, (2) feminists, (3) women's equality agencies, and (4) neoliberals—all of which are addressed in this book (Farris, 2017). These groups use native informants like Hirsi Ali and Eltahawy to portray Islam as a misogynistic religion and culture, enabling the philosophy "West over the rest." Much like Lewis and Ajami, femonationalism aids Western governments in justifying wars by presenting Islam through a fear-mongering lens with "an authentic Muslim woman's voice" (Mahmood, 2003).

Femonationalism is reminiscent of Oriental feminism—"a type of feminism that advocates and supports particular foreign policies toward the Middle East" (Bahramitash, 2005, 221). What femonationalism encompasses that Oriental feminism does not is rhetoric that not only encourages certain actions abroad but also campaigns against a multicultural society within the West that includes Islamic practices—such as veiling. Femonationalism argues that if women in Iran do not want to wear hijab, then why should the United States work to normalize hijab. Femonationalism claims that because women are liberated in the Western world, allowing misogynistic practices like veiling threatens the West's emancipatory nature—or, in the case of France, its secular culture.

Yet, while the West is certainly situated within a patriarchal framework, femonationalists and native informants have successfully deflected away from Western culture's forms of inequality against women. Eltahawy's (2012) article in *Foreign Policy* magazine illustrates her contempt for Islam and Arab men, stating that "the Islamist hatred of women burns brightly across the region." Additionally, Eltahawy acknowledges that women struggle regardless of where they live (including the United States) but argues that regardless of how Western countries are treating their women, Arab nations are doing far worse. She writes:

> But let's put aside what the United States does or does not do to women. Name me an Arab country, and I'll recite a litany of abuses fueled by a toxic mix of culture, and religion that few seem willing or able to disentangle lest they blaspheme or offend.

Strangely, while Eltahawy is an avid critic of the patriarchy, she characterizes Muslim men in a circle of their own—beyond general patriarchal evils. Western feminism has latched on to this narrative and continues to showcase Muslim women as victims both dangerous to American values yet vulnerable to Islamic brainwashing (Mohanty, 1991; Terman, 2017; Hasan, 2018). Furthermore, Western feminism tends to recognize specific forms of "feminist" practice, which include protesting in the streets, exposing one's body, or fighting on the frontlines (Mohanty, 1991; Fernandez, 2013).

While Arab and Muslim women have engaged in these practices, they are not limited by Western interpretations of feminism, especially when it comes to veiling. Veiling in an Islamic context is a point of obsession in the West, and, in many instances, context is absent from the discourse. Rather than acknowledge the religious, cultural, and sacred practice, the predominant narrative surrounding the veil is political and associated with repression (Heath, 2008). The contention surrounding the veil can cause confusion among Western feminists, especially when hijab is used as a form of resistance. Regardless of that misunderstanding, there are certainly instances where women do wear hijab as a symbol of resistance either in accordance with or absent from religious purposes. McGinty's (2014) study on the "Emotional Geographies of Veiling" showed that many women in the United States wear hijab as a form of activism in an attempt to normalize hijab and combat Islamophobic narratives. Linda Sarsour, a Palestinian-American activist and co-organizer of the Women's March, did not come from a strict Muslim family, and she did not start wearing the hijab until she was twenty years old, by her own choice. She says, "[The hijab] gives me a visible identity . . . when people ask, 'what are you?' at least there's one thing I don't have to explain. And it's a journey towards a spiritual identity that I'm proud of" (Abrahamian, April 27, 2017, para 17). Sarsour's experience is interesting to consider within this context as she recognizes hijab as a choice, not a compulsion.

While some feminists in the West accept and support hijab, many still do not. In fact, some countries, like France, have implemented various bans on hijab, claiming that the practice contradicts the free and secular nature of the West. Hijab is a tangible way to recognize Muslim women, and because a narrative describing Muslim women as oppressed exists, the removal of the hijab has come to be recognized as a way to liberate those women not only from brown men but also from themselves. Additionally, those women who are willing to remove hijab prove their loyalty to the nation state and rebuke the suspicion of them as a security threat (Amir-Khan, 2012). However, while some Western governments claim that they are rescuing women from the fate that is Islam by denying women the right to wear the veil, these authorities are actually practicing subjugation rather than emancipation (Heath, 2008). Though, with the help of native informants, femonationalist rhetoric continues to spread with little to no pushback. Additionally, the more native informants' work and voices are amplified in mainstream news media, the more legitimacy they earn. Likewise, well-meaning feminists can also perpetuate credibility for femonationalists by engaging in the homogenizing image of the Muslim woman.

TRANSNATIONAL FEMINISM AND
SOLIDARITY WITH MUSLIM WOMEN

Transnational feminism can be complex when performing actions of solidarity. This particularly becomes an issue when Western women make efforts to transcend physical boundaries through digital activism to show solidarity with Muslim women. While paved with good intentions, often white or Western feminism homogenizes the experiences of Muslim women and remains unaware of the geographical nuances that exist within those lived experiences (Mohanty, 2003). This mindset is somewhat understandable considering that much of the Western discourse on Muslim women's lived experience is rooted in stories from native informants.

In the case of Muslim women, colonial feminism has illustrated an infatuation with the veil (Abu-Lughod, 2013), both advocating for and protesting it. For example, in 2017, Shepard Fairey collaborated with Munira Ahmed to create an iconic image of the Muslim American woman. Fairey is best known for his iconic image of Barack Obama featured on campaign posters offering a message of hope. However, the reasoning behind this new project served as a response to the then president-elect Donald Trump's racist rhetoric throughout his campaign. The image features Ahmed wearing the American flag as a hijab with the caption, "We the People." Ahmed explained that the message behind the image is about saying, "I am American and I am Muslim, and I am very proud of both" (Helmore, 2017, para. 3). However, the illustration proved to be quite controversial among American Muslim women, including New York City journalist Ghazala Irshad who believes the image sends an uncomfortable message about nationalism. She says,

> I see the image of a Muslim woman wearing the American flag as a hijab as problematic [. . .] I believe in the freedom of choice for a woman to wear it or not wear it. But I do want the media, or an artist creating a narrative about us to recognize that we don't all wear hijabs, and there is diversity in this community that is being ignored. (McCluskey, 2017, para. 8)

What Irshad is suggesting is that the image of the American flag hijab neglects the intersectionality of Muslim women (Yuval-Davis, 2015) and instead perpetuates reductionist depictions of Muslim women that reduce them to hijab and present them as victims; not to mention, there is a complete oversight of non-hijabi Muslim women. This restrained framework reduces Muslim women to hijab and ignores all other Islamic practices (Gokariksel and Smith, 2017). Following tragic events like the Christchurch shooting in New Zealand, several women and children in Auckland wore headscarves as a sign of solidarity with Muslim women. When asked why, one woman, Bell Sibly, replied, "Well, my primary reason was that if anybody else turns up waving a gun, I want to stand between him and anybody he might be pointing it at. And I don't want him to be able to tell the difference, because there is no difference" (Taylor and Kanso, 2019). Again, while Sibly's actions were well-intended, her choices illicit an important debate on the relationship between solidarity and identity. Arnesperger and Varoufakis (2003) define solidarity as a person's ability to identify with another's condition and/or experience, separating it from terms like altruism and charity. Yet, Featherstone (2012) challenges this definition to some degree. In Featherstone's (2012) theoretical take on solidarity, there is no pre-requisite of similarity in identity or experience. Rather, solidarity is the taking up of a political struggle to dispute oppression and inequality.

Within Featherstone's framework, white/Western non-Muslim women's donning of the hijab may not constitute solidarity but rather, as Azadi (2015) argues, a form of cultural appropriation. While Azadi (2015) acknowledges the altruistic motivations behind non-Muslim women wearing the hijab, she challenges those seeking to show true solidarity with Muslim women to rethink their actions. Azadi's (2015) use of the term "solidarity" is understood to be an effort "to build relationships of *mutual* aid. In this way, one does not act simply on conscience, but interrogates why an inequitable relation exists in the first place." Azadi's (2015) utilization of solidarity speaks to Barnett and Land's (2007) "geographies of generosity" in which "caring from a distance" does not necessarily promote altruistic intentions but rather encourages partiality and self-interest—meaning those that care from afar advocate for campaigns that support their own ideologies and serve as a "modality of power."

Rahbari (2019) makes a similar argument saying, "humanitarian frameworks are not free from relations of power and can be interpreted as inhabiting colonialist attitudes" (11). Non-Muslim Western women have to ask themselves how their attempts at solidarity affect the community they are supporting. For instance, what does wearing the hijab for reasons of solidarity communicate to women whose experience with mandatory hijab is painful or humiliating?" (Azadi, 2015). So, how then can Western feminists advocate for Muslim women? Azadi (2015) suggests:

> I think that we can choose paths of solidarity without having to appropriate or become the people or things we are in solidarity with. Instead, making and/or giving space to marginalized communities to speak for themselves is often the best way to ally.

The best way to be an ally for Muslim women is to recognize their agency—something American news media can easily do by providing space on its pages and airwaves for Muslim women to speak for themselves rather than relying on anecdotal evidence from native informants. Furthermore, feminists must resist the urge to speak for Muslim women, lest they continue to perpetuate liberal feminist imperialism. By taking the Western voice out of the discourse and allowing Muslim women to speak for themselves about their own lived experiences (as they are the only ones qualified to do so), transnational feminism can best be embodied. Genuine solidarity, as defined by Azadi—providing a platform for women to speak their truth—will serve as the interpretation used within the context of this text.

As discussed, Western media portray Islam as a religion that is violent against women and, thus, an inevitable part of the culture of Islamic states. This victimhood often manifests itself in the West's obsession with veiling, a narrative present in both domestic and international politics without acknowledging the historical context of veiling (Seddighi and Tafakori, 2016). While recognizing state-gendered violence and discrimination against Arab and Muslim women is vital and warranted, often Western mainstream news shift their focus away from state-gendered violence and toward violence dictated by Islam, with the help of native informants (Abu-Lughod, 2013). Femonationalism feeds off these narratives and continues to demonize Islam and Muslim men while also patronizing Arab and Muslim women. Because those same narratives continue to play out in American mainstream news media, there is an implication that the media (all across the political spectrum) are complicit in perpetuating femonationalist discourse. Femonationalist discourse subsequently translates into a fear that the American audience internalizes, thus sustaining Islamophobia in the United States.

Chapter 5

Methodology

This book explores U.S. news media and Twitter discourse surrounding the #WhiteWednesdays campaign specifically by using critical discourse analysis. As discussed in the previous chapters, former research has shown that Western news media discourse tends to project orientalist tropes on Arab and Muslim women (Mishra, 2007; Terman, 2017; Kumar, 2018) or promote a "multicultural feminism" that ignores the "cultural and economic inequities of globalization" (Shome, 2006, 255). However, transnational feminist scholars are contributing to media studies by addressing issues of power on a global scale. Transnational feminism within media studies engages the "larger social imaginations" surrounding representations of gender to track the evolution of how gender is articulated in globalization and how certain narratives are reproduced (257). Specifically, this case study asks: To what extent does the news discourse and the Twitter discourse on #WhiteWednesdays reflect transnational feminism, femonationalism, and/or orientalist narratives?

Critical discourse analysis (CDA) is an ideal method for this analysis because it helps link discursive practices to their ideological sources and unpack the power relations within those practices. Furthermore, CDA also addresses the social and political consequences of discursive practices while operating with a tendency to work on behalf of oppressed groups. CDA does not pretend to be an "objective" scientific method as the researcher examines discourses with the explicit purpose of uncovering the ideological structures behind those discourses that empower some but not others. Additionally, CDA analyzes discourse through the lens of societal power structures and works to reveal the ideological roots and social consequences of those discourses (Barkho, 2011).

For example, in Khosravnik and Sarkoh's (2017) study on Arabism and anti-Persian sentiments, the authors use CDA to analyze social media discourse "to explore the construction of an imagined pan-Arabic identity versus its regional rival, the Persian identity" (3614). The authors argue that "the relationship between discourse and context is dialectical and interdependent" and specifically used Reisigl and Wodak's (2009) discourse-historical approach that focuses on the "mediation between language (microfeatures of discourse) and society (macrostructures surrounding discourse)" (3619). By utilizing this approach, the authors were able to establish discursive themes by first analyzing linguistic characteristics of the text and then interpreting the text within the larger societal context.

In another study by Lawless and Chen (2016), the authors focus on the international news discourses surrounding the movements "Occupy" and the Arab Spring to examine how ideologies are discursively reproduced. Lawless and Chen (2016) first reconceptualize the two social movements as "discursive formations" (Foucault, 1972)—"discourses that belong in a single knowledge system, despite an apparent disconnection or segregated conceptualization" and analyze how those formations reproduce hegemonic ideologies (186). They utilize Fairclough's (2003) approach to CDA with a multilevel analysis of the text, followed by linking the text to wider societal practices. The noteworthy element of this study's methodology is the focus on interdiscursivity—"when different discourses and genres are articulated together in a communicative event" (Jorgensen and Phillips, 2002, 73). In this study, language used to describe the Occupy movement often drew from comparisons to the Arab Spring, which allowed the authors to analyze the text as it relates to sociocultural practices.

Much like Lawless and Chen's (2016) study, CDA within media studies (van Dijk, 1997; Fairclough, 2003) has primarily focused on mass communication and traditional media sources "because of their normalizing power to frame, centralize, and legitimize particular views" (Lawless and Chen, 2016, 185). While mainstream news media is recognized as powerful and its narratives hegemonic, this case study will focus primarily on user-generated content from social media platforms alongside mainstream news content. This case study augments the use of CDA by specifically focusing on "bottom-up" discursive practices that concentrate on content from ordinary prosumers on Twitter. By examining mainstream news narratives alongside user-generated content, there is the benefit to utilize interdiscursivity as both discourses draw from one another. Focusing on user-generated content by the subjects covered in mainstream news narratives, this case study uses CDA to highlight the discursive practices used by women activists to reaffirm or challenge hegemonic discourses.

As it relates to transnational feminist scholarship, examining the conversation between mainstream news media and Arab and Muslim women activists on Twitter is consistent with transnational feminists' pursuit to decolonize knowledge production by (1) challenging the gender bias of male leadership in social movements; (2) producing alternative histories that privilege voices from the margins; and (3) highlighting shifting meanings of cultural symbols (Grewal and Kaplan, 1994; Basu, 1995; Moghadam, 2000; Mohanty, 2003; Fernandez, 2012; Falcón, 2016; Farris, 2017). Analyzing the Twitter discourse as it relates to mainstream news narratives also brings context to the news commentary (that would otherwise be absent), protects the audience from misinformation, and highlights women's stories being told on their own terms (Mislán and Shaban, 2018). Research indicates that digital social movements have allowed for protesters to construct their own identities, form collective identities, and establish affective social networks that intensify the digital public sphere (Gerbaudo and Trere, 2015; Papacharissi, 2015; Davidson, Bondi and Smith 2016). By exploring the discourses of Iranian protesters on Twitter, this case study contributes to critical theorists' goal of disrupting hegemonic narratives. By allowing Twitter users to utilize that social space to reconstruct their bodies and identities they can challenge those hegemonic narratives in mainstream media (Lee, 2017) and, in this case, the traditional foreign policy efforts between the United States and the Middle East that inevitably shape women's rights initiatives within the region.

EXPLORING TWITTER DISCOURSE

The #WhiteWednesdays campaign was inspired by events on the ground and was circulated via social media which cultivated the transnational nature of these movements. Social media platforms can be a public sphere for both men and women to engage in dialogue, which is especially important when women exist in spaces that are segregated by sex. On Twitter, they can engage in the "sphere of autonomy" (Castells, 2015)—a space that challenges authoritarian regimes' ability to censor content online (Douai, 2013; Zayani, 2018). Twitter discourse enables women with the tools to cross borders in places where their freedom of mobility is limited by guardianship laws, driving bans, and discrimination on the basis of sex (Zayani, 2018). The platform also allows women the freedom to challenge hegemonic narratives within the mainstream domestically and abroad (Grewal and Kaplan, 1994). Within this space, women involved in these campaigns can speak for themselves and confront misattributions of their resistance to a particular consciousness or politics (Mahmood, 2004). However, this is not to suggest that new media enables freedom (Khondker, 2011; Fenton, 2016, 49). Rather the ways users repurpose internet technologies are what encourages liberation and what constitutes as alternative/activist new media (Lievrow, 2011).

The sample for this study was obtained using Twitter's Application Programming Interface (API)—which allows access to all public tweets. The author searched for the hashtag #WhiteWednesdays and started with a data set containing 4,925 original tweets (no replies, retweets, or quotes) from December 28, 2017–January 10, 2020. These data identify the author, time of tweet, and the content of the tweet. Furthermore, this study focused on Iranian/Iranian American voices and concentrated on tweets from those voices. I relied on a user's Twitter bio and/or language used in the tweet (i.e., Persian) to determine if the user identified as an Iranian or an Iranian American (Hermida et al., 2014, 49).

The Twitter data for this study was narrowed down to using "critical discourse moments"—"periods that involve specific happenings, which may challenge the 'established' discursive positions" (Carvalho, 2008, 166). However, this study was not limited to the data originally generated by the hashtag. Following Tinati, Halford, Carr and Pope's (2014) approach to Twitter analysis within social research, the author examined "the emergence of a communications network, and have explored which users and which information rise to the surface as a result of a dynamic flow of information" (676). Critical discourse moments are a great starting point to trace the actors and connections that emerged within the network of White Wednesdays. Beginning with Viva Movahed's act of protest on December 27, 2017, the following critical discourse moments guide this case study:

July 5, 2018 Masih Alinejad tweeted the following:

> I'm giving an interview to an #Italian magazine about Federica Mogherini who betrayed #Iranian people, especially #women, for the sake of the nuclear deal which only benefited the regime. @FedericaMog

The tweet was accompanied by a photo of European Union Foreign Policy Chief Federica Mogherini with her head covered by a scarf, while meeting with the president of Iran, Hassan Rouhani. Mogherini's decision to wear a headscarf while on a diplomatic visit to Iran received backlash from Alinejad as well as other activists. Alinejad argued that European women leaders that choose to comply with compulsory hijab are hurting the Iranian women's cause (Maloney and Katz, 2019). Alinejad has since appeared publicly condemning Mogherini's actions, including an interview with the Italian magazine she references in her tweet.

February 4, 2019 Masih Alinejad tweets the following:

> I am officially announcing that I am meeting with @SecPompeo to tell him how on the 40th anniversary of Islamic Republic, a significant number of Iranians

want this oppressive regime to be gone. Read my full statement in the link below:

#Iran/#WhiteWendesdays

According to the White House (2019), Alinejad did meet with Pompeo on February 4, 2019, sparking controversy on her decision to appeal to the United States, a known adversary of Iran.

March 6, 2019 Nasrin Sotoudeh, an Iranian human rights lawyer, is arrested for "several national security-related offenses" (BBC, 2019). Sotoudeh is well known for representing Iranian women who have been jailed for removing their headscarves. Sotoudeh was initially sentenced to thirty-eight years in prison but was eventually only called to serve a maximum of twelve years. According to the BBC, Sotoudeh was a former political prisoner as well as the recipient of the Sakharov Prize for Freedom of Thought by the European Parliament.

May 9, 2019 Masih Alinejad testified before the Canadian Foreign Affairs Committee regarding whether sanctions targeting the Islamic Revolutionary Guard Corps (IRGC) would be helpful or harmful to the Iranian people. According to a transcript provided by OpenParliament.CA (2019), Alinejad responded with the following:

I support targeted sanctions, and I want to make clear that, yes, general sanctions hurt Iranian people. Ordinary people are suffering from general sanctions. However, targeted sanctions sanctioning Sepah, the revolutionary guard and Iranian national TV are what the Iranian people want, because these are the main propaganda tools.

May 12, 2019 Masih Alinejad tweets the following:

It's shameful that Western diplomats like Véronique Petit go to Iran & wear compulsory hijab unhesitatingly. Meanwhile, #WhiteWednesdays activists like #Yasaman_aryani, her mother & #Mojgan_keshavarz are in prison for removing compulsory hijab. How about their experiences?

The tweet is accompanied by a retweet showcasing the ambassador in hijab while visiting Iran. It should be noted that Petit was the first woman elected to ambassador for both Saudi Arabia and Iran, two countries notorious for their oppression against women.

January 6, 2020 Ilhan Omar retweeted an article criticizing Masih Alinejad for being a Voice of America (VOA) journalist, for being a U.S. government contractor as well as calling her a propaganda tool for U.S. President Trump. The retweet was accompanied by a confused emoji. It should be noted that Alinejad publicly supported the U.S. killing of Qassem Soleimani, an Iranian general for the IRGC (see table 5.1).

Miscellaneous tweets featured at the bottom of the chart indicate those tweets which were found and analyzed by searching the threads of the original published. The integral tweets are important to incorporate in the sample as they exemplify how conversations surrounding #WhiteWednesdays evolved into discourses focused on larger social practices within feminism and Islam—a key component of CDA. The tweets included in the discourse analysis were chosen after reviewing all of the 4,925 tweets in the original data set. They were chosen based on their rich contribution to the discourse on #WhiteWednesdays.

EXPLORING MAINSTREAM NEWS DISCOURSE

Mainstream news media stories focused on the #WhiteWednesdays campaign are richer for analysis when coupled with the Twitter discourse. Despite ideological differences, mainstream news, within this context, will be defined as "monolithic," "profit-making," exclusive hierarchal institutions (Downing, 1984). By analyzing the mainstream and alternative discourses alongside each other, there is more room to explore the nuances, challenges, misconceptions, and validations within each narrative. In recent years, more and more Americans are citing online platforms and phone apps as their preferred source of news, with television standing as the number-one preferred source (Pew Research Center, 2019). For example, "CNN was the most popular news brand among mobile only users in 2018, with 28.4 million consumers accessing CNN's content exclusively via mobile" (Watson, 2019). Due to this evolution, the mainstream news data for this

Table 5.1   Critical Discourse Moments

Date	Event	Tweets Analyzed
December 27, 2017	Movahed Protests	15
July 5, 2018	Alinejad's Interview—Federica	15
February 4, 2019	Alinejad Announces Meeting w/Pompeo	31
March 6, 2019	Sotoudeh Arrested	29
May 9, 2019	Alinejad Testifies Before Canadian FCA	5
May 12, 2019	Ambassador Petite Arrives in Iran in Hijab	8
January 10, 2020	Omar Attacks Alinejad on Twitter	15
Integral Tweets		41
TOTAL		159

study included online articles and interviews from six of the most popular news outlets in the United States including *USA Today, Fox News Channel, The Washington Post, The New York Times, CNN,* and *The Wall Street Journal.*

USA Today currently holds 3 million daily readers and has acquired 102.2 million unique visitors to USAToday.com since June 2017. The paper's audience generally consists of a mixed ideological base, with some leaning more toward the left. *The New York Times* is the largest seven-day newspaper in the United States and currently ranks as number one in the overall reach of U.S. opinion leaders. *The New York Times* is also the United States' newspaper of record. The paper's audience tends to lean ideologically from left to center. *The Wall Street Journal* is the United States' leading business publication and reaches 22.4 million digital readers per month. The paper's audience is roughly evenly distributed ideologically (Business Insider, 2014). *The Washington Post* reported 71.8 million unique visitors monthly in April 2019 with 86.6 million unique visitors in March 2019 alone (WashPost PR, 2019). The paper was purchased by Jeff Bezos in 2013 and is reported to hold a mostly liberal political stance (Pew Research Center, 2014). CNN, established in 1980, was the first news network to establish the twenty-four-hour news cycle. As of October 2019, CNN.com stands as the number-one online news destination. The news outlet is reported to hold a leftist political stance (Pew Research Center, 2014).

The final news outlet included in this study is *Fox News*—an outlet holding a unique position within this sample as it is the only right-winged political news outlet. In 2019, *Fox News* had an average audience of 2.5 million viewers (Joyella, 2019) and currently stands as the number-one most-watched cable news network in the United States (Pasley, 2019). While *Fox News* claims to be in opposition to mainstream news media, according to Noam Chomsky's (1997) definition of mainstream news as agenda-setting outlets with extensive access to resources; "major, very profitable corporations [. . .] they are way up at the top of the power structure of the private economy which is a very tyrannical structure." The network's success can be credited to its former CEO, Roger Ailes. However, *Fox News* does differ from mainstream news in its deliberate decision not to separate fact from opinion as well as its distinct and vocal support for the Trump administration. The network has enjoyed a mutually beneficial relationship with the president, with *Fox News* consistently advocating for Trump's presidency as well as Trump's public amplification of *Fox News* on Twitter. In light of the Trump administration's relationship with the media outlet, *Fox News* was included in this study to observe if/how reporters used their platform to support the administration's appropriation of the #WhiteWednesdays campaign and, therefore, perpetuate a specific political agenda.

The author examined fifty-one news articles/interviews using the following search terms: Iran, compulsory hijab. The timeframe for this search is December 28, 2017–January 13, 2020—beginning from the date Viva Movahed stood on the utility box in Tehran to the start of this study (see table 5.2).

While the majority of the news outlets included in this study fall in the centrist/leftist ideological camps (with the exception of *Fox News*), this study is not fixated on liberal versus conservative narratives. Rather, this study focuses on the dominant news narratives—leading the author to select news outlets based on circulation. Furthermore, while the sample consists of fifty-one articles/interviews (everything available during the time period selected for this study), these articles/interviews are rich in content and ideal units of analysis for CDA.

DATA PROCESS

This study took both an ideological and discursive approach to analysis, specifically examining how social practice creates and reproduces power. This is a critical aspect of CDA as Barkho (2011) argues, "the social and discursive practices of media institutions is different from the social and discursive reality of other components of our social world" (301). The model for the study combined Khosravnik and Sarkoh's (2017), and Lawless and Chen's (2016) approach to CDA—the former approach for the Twitter data set and the latter approach for the mainstream news data.

The approach to the Twitter data begins with examining the data set as a whole and noting the timelines when Twitter activity was higher than usual. Noting those timelines, the author investigated events related to #WhiteWednesdays and developed a list of critical discourse moments when arguments changed or when new/alterative ones emerged. After developing the critical discourse moments, the author read through the tweets surrounding each critical discourse moment. Additionally, if a tweet received extensive replies, the author read through the thread in order to access the organic network emerging from the #WhiteWednesdays campaign. After collecting a data set for each critical discourse moment, I did an open coding on each individual data set to develop initial codes and analytical categories based on the femonationalist and transnational feminist frameworks.

Table 5.2   Mainstream News Sample

News	USAToday	FoxNews	WashPo	NYTimes	CNN	WSJ	Total
Articles	8	7	11	13	10	2	51

After establishing codes, the author conducted another analysis consisting of all the data sets associated with each critical discourse moment. During this stage of analysis, the author examined the objects/ideas presented in each tweet. For example, tweets that referred to "true feminism" or the function of "hijab" were considered discursively constructed objects/ideas. Additionally, the author noted the actors featured in each tweet. For example, who was tweeting the most? Which actors were mentioned the most? How were those actors represented? Whose perspective appeared to dominate the discourse? Furthermore, the author also analyzed the discursive strategies present in the Twitter discourse—framing, selection, and composition, positioning, legitimation, and politicization.

For the mainstream news data, this study adopted Fairclough's (1992) approach to CDA—a multilevel analysis of texts linked to wider social practices to reveal discursive strategies regarding power, agency, and hegemony. The analysis included the following steps: (1) analyzing the function of the text; (2) interrogating the discursive practices of the text; and (3) explaining the text's relation to wider societal ideologies (Lawless and Chen, 189). Using CDA in this research revealed the hegemonic ideologies embedded within mainstream U.S. news media and affirmed the discursive strategies used by women's activists in the #WhiteWednesdays movements. Additionally, using CDA allowed for the exploration of interdiscursivity between the news texts and the Twitter texts. By employing interdiscursivity, this study included how the news texts and tweets interacted, responded, and exploited one another.

Chapter 6

News Coverage Analysis

The sample news coverage of #WhiteWednesdays included articles and interviews from *USA Today*, *Fox News*, *The Washington Post*, *The New York Times*, *CNN*, and *The Wall Street Journal*. In an open reading of the text, there was a noticeable lack of diversity among sources—only two television segments featured women from the #WhiteWednesdays campaign apart from activist and exiled Iranian journalist Masih Alinejad. While the ideological stances slightly wavered across the news sources, with *The New York Times* operating under the most transnational paradigm, the overarching discourse revealed similar ideological positions.

The discourse across all the news sources created a binary narrative on hijab, perpetuating an "us vs. them" narrative that depicted sources as either for or against hijab while simultaneously overlooking the core issue—a woman's right to choose. The "us vs. them" framework extended to a battlefield in which Muslim women from the global South were pitted against Muslim women in the global North, projecting a divided front on the role of hijab in feminism. Secondly, the lack of public support from Muslim American women for the women of #WhiteWednesdays created an opportunity for right-wing news media to broadcast femonationalist rhetoric by portraying inclusive steps for hijabi women in the United States as trivial in comparison to the life-threatening issues facing women in Iran protesting compulsory hijab. Additionally, across all of the news outlets, the women in Iran were consistently described using empowering language (i.e., brave, warriors, strong)—a sharp contrast to how news media have reported on Muslim women in the past (Mishra, 2007; Terman, 2017). Of course, while this discourse employed language that seemingly depicted the Iranian activists as empowered, such rhetoric also aligned with the geopolitical interests of the United States—more of which will be discussed later. Moreover, throughout the news discourse, the language is essentially a modernized version of an orientalist narrative used as a conduit to promote Western economic and political interests (Said, 1978).

Notably, the discourse on #WhiteWednesdays was almost entirely shaped by Masih Alinejad and other elevated voices within the Muslim feminist movement—namely Linda Sarsour and Ilhan Omar—all three elitist sources. The politics of representation present within the discourse proved problematic as one woman cannot represent all of the women in Iran just as one American hijabi woman cannot represent all hijabi women in the United States. More importantly, Iranian women's voices on the ground were lost within the debates on the hijab among the privileged voices of women in power. Without the grassroots voices of #WhiteWednesdays, the campaign's transnational elements became obsolete, again, laying the groundwork for femonationalism to appropriate the movement.

A BINARY NARRATIVE ON HIJAB: MASIH ALINEJAD AND LINDA SARSOUR FACE OFF ON CNN

The news media discourse surrounding #WhiteWednesdays focused on the issue of mutual exclusivity between hijab and feminism. This discourse was primarily dictated by Alinejad likely because (a) she initiated the #WhiteWednesdays movement as an offshoot of her original campaign My Stealthy Freedom, which lends her a sense of credibility and authority; and (b) she lives in Brooklyn. Carvalho (2008) calls this "framing power"—an actor's ability to communicate their views via media, specifically through journalists (168). Alinejad's framing power extended beyond granting interviews to journalists and included the publication of her own news articles, including two pieces in *The Washington Post*—"There are two types of hijabs. The difference is huge," coauthored with Iranian American journalist Roya Hakakian (April 2019), and "Don't believe Iranian propaganda about the mourning for Soleimani" (January 2020) as well as a piece in *The Wall Street Journal* titled, "My Brother Ali is Iran's latest hostage." Alinejad's op-eds are reminiscent of those Bernard Lewis wrote for *The Wall Street Journal*, *The New Yorker*, and *The Atlantic*.

The focus on the constitution of both hijab and feminism monopolized the news media discourse, again, largely through the voice of Alinejad. Alinejad used discursive strategies to manipulate the reality of #WhiteWednesdays by juxtaposing progressive measures with hijab against oppressive experiences with hijab. For example, in February 2018, the department store Macy's decided to start stocking a luxury hijab brand, "The Verona Collection"—a brand that celebrates "women's empowerment and taking pride in one's

Muslim identity" (Vogl, 2021). The decision came after Nike released a "Pro-Hijab" for Muslim athletes, and American Eagle released an exclusive denim hijab that sold out. Macy's decision was supported by some and criticized by others. In light of this disagreement, *CNN* invited Alinejad and Linda Sarsour, a Palestinian-American civil rights activist, to debate the issue and discuss the politicization of the hijab. The Macy's story quickly shifted to the protests against the compulsory hijab in Iran. Alinejad used the platform to negate the hijab as a symbol of resistance as well as to call out Western feminists, saying, "We shouldn't let any feminists in the West downplay our cause and say this is a small issue, it's not." Sarsour responded by arguing that the real issue at hand is the narrative surrounding hijab—particularly the assertion that American Muslim women wearing hijab are "upholding a system of oppression." However, while Sarsour plainly stated her solidarity with the women in Iran, she also called for those same women "to create a narrative that says you also stand with my right as a Muslim woman in America who is having to endure Islamophobia" (Scott, 2018). Sarsour's response stems from her conviction to eradicate Islamophobic harassment against American Muslim women who wear hijab. While she uses this televised platform to publicly state that she supports the women in Iran protesting, she also communicates that her support is conditional. Sarsour's solidarity is somewhat contingent on whether women in Iran will also show solidarity with Muslim women in America subject to Islamophobia. Like Alinejad, Sarsour's discourse is also tied to the politics of Islam; only her narrative exclusively reflects the interests of Muslim women in the United States.

Alinejad's rebuttal was simple: "you cannot use the same tool which is the most visible symbol of oppression in the Middle East and say that this is a sign of resistance [in the United States]." In this statement alone, Alinejad negates any transnational feminist narrative associated with the #WhiteWednesdays campaign because she refused to recognize the politics of location associated with the hijab (Rich, 1984). Alinejad's rhetoric reflects that of the native informant and continues to demonize the hijab as a threat to secularization and modernity. Sarsour concluded the debate by equating the oppression Iranian women face with those of Muslim American women stating that "a woman in Iran takes the risk of not wearing hijab based on the laws there and has to risk that—we in the United States, Muslim women, risk wearing hijab" (Scott, 2018). Sarsour's point speaks to the problematic hierarchy of oppression. One Muslim woman's struggle does not negate the others.

Within this conversation, the issue of Macy's decision to sell hijabs was discussed in conjunction with the protests against compulsory hijab in Iran—a discourse deliberately orchestrated by a *CNN* producer. The invitation extended to Sarsour to participate in the conversation is a privileged one as she has become a well-known political figure since the 2018 Women's

March. Furthermore, Sarsour holds a controversial reputation for wearing the hijab as a symbol of her identity and empowerment—an ideal representative to be pitted against a woman leading the charge against compulsory hijab. In this context, Sarsour supposedly represents Muslim American women—or at least those that choose to wear the hijab as those are the only women she refers to in this segment. Sarsour advocates for the right to choose to wear the hijab, and she is the only woman in her family that wears one. She made the choice when she was nineteen to express her Muslim identity. Ironically, Alinejad is the only one in her family that does not wear the hijab to illustrate her own identity. Theoretically, she represents Iranian women—or at least those against compulsory hijab if not the practice of hijab altogether.

Sarsour uses language that equates the lived experience of hijabi women in the United States with those of Iranian women—bypassing the contextual elements. While hijab in the United States is not illegal, it can attract Islamophobic harassment. Meanwhile, in Iran, it is unlawful for women to be seen in public without hijab, and it is punishable by law through beatings or arrest. However, Alinejad corroborates the orientalist discourse on hijab, which lends femonationalist rhetoric a false sense of legitimacy by not acknowledging the nuances of hijab. The lack of nuance allows Alinejad the opportunity to frame Sarsour as a Western feminist diminishing women's lived experience in Iran. In both discourses, the politics of location (Rich, 1984; Mohanty, 2003) is neglected. Instead, the binary narrative, in which Sarsour represents "pro-hijab" and Alinejad represents "anti-hijab," oversimplifies the broader issue of women's choice for the audience (Rich, 1984; Mohanty, 2003). As long as the news narrative presents this as a binary issue, audience members are likely to accept it as a binary issue—particularly when two well-known activists reinforce that discourse.

The Macy's story also became a contention point during a *Fox News* talk show, *Tucker Carlson Tonight*. Carlson opens his segment on Macy's by referring to the hijab as "Muslim garb consistent with Sharia Law"—already ignoring the nuances surrounding hijab. He notes that while the rising Muslim population in the West raises issues of "social cohesion and national security," it is also "influencing fashion" (Wells, 2018). Before the interview with his guest even begins, Carlson opens the conversation by framing Macy's decision as a Muslim takeover rather than a step toward a more inclusive society—ignoring Macy's struggle to keep their heads above water after closing 100 stores in 2016. Hedge (2011) speaks to Carlson's behavior in which the use of gender issues is continuously used to promote "social and political agendas"—specifically, using rhetoric on veiling as a tool to illustrate "widespread resistance to Muslim migration" (p. 3). In this case, Carlson has an entire show to broadcast resistance to Muslim migration, starting with the hijab. Carlson goes on to interview his guest, the New York branch of

NOW (the National Organization for Women) Sonia Ossario. Ossario immediately acknowledges that Macy's decision was unlikely to be a political one but rather a response to a report stating that Muslim women, globally, hold $44 billion in buying power.

Macy's was not the first American company to pursue a hijab fashion line—Nike, Dolce and Gabbana, Burberry, H&M, and Zara are just a few of the fashion companies taking advantage of what the *New York Times* called, "a lucrative Muslim clothing market" in Caron and Salam's (2018) article titled "Macy's courts Muslims with new hijab brand." In the article, Caron and Salam (2018) cite the Global Islamic Economy Report stating that globally, in 2016 alone, $245 billion was spent on Muslim attire, and the market is predicted to be worth $373 billion by 2022. Additionally, according to the American Muslim Consortium, Muslim spending power in the United States is purported at $100 billion.

While *The New York Times* recognizes what the hijab market can do for the U.S. economy, Caron and Salam (2018) do not shy away from the problematic circumstances involving hijab around the world. They reference the women in Iran protesting compulsory hijab as well as women in France who were harassed or altogether banned from wearing hijab, veils, burqas, and the controversial burkini. Additionally, the reporters explore the discourse presented by hijabi fashion bloggers worldwide, providing nuance to the narratives surrounding the hijab. Overall, Caron and Salam (2018) incorporate nuance, context, and conflicting discourses for the audience to consider, unlike the discourses found within the *Fox News* coverage.

In another article from *The New York Times*, "Mediating Faith and Style," Finkel (2018) reports on a new exhibition at San Francisco's de Young Museum focusing on contemporary Muslim fashion. The exhibit received much backlash, including accusations of "celebrating the oppression of women" as well as Muslims arguing that "the notion of 'fashion' is antithetical to the religion's modest dress codes." Finkel (2018) asked the museum's director how he navigated such a sensitive topic, especially with events like #WhiteWednesdays emerging. The director responded by referencing his culturally sensitive curators, including a professor of cultural studies at the London College of Fashion and leading expert on modest fashion, Reina Lewis. Lewis immediately denounced the exhibit's working title "The Fashion of Islam" saying, "I would never talk about Muslim fashion in the singular and expect it to be just one thing." Additionally, Lewis "invited dozens of Muslim representatives from local universities, Islamic centers and mosques to consult on the show," which introduced the curators to the different perspectives on the hijab and its myths serving exclusively as a symbol of oppression. Finkel's (2018) article borrows from the same paradigm as Caron and Salam's (2018) reporting that illustrates the overall approach from

The New York Times on the constitution of the hijab during the time of the #WhiteWednesdays protests—a transnational paradigm.

In the examples above from *CNN*, *Fox News*, and *The New York Times*, reporters from all three outlets addressed Macy's business decision in juxtaposition to the #WhiteWednesdsays protests—creating a spectacle focused on the role of hijab as opposed to the role of the women affected by these events. *CNN* brought Alinejad and Sarsour together to debate the hijab's role in resistance in which Sarsour advocated for a Muslim woman's right to choose to wear hijab. At the same time, Alinejad primarily focused on the negative aspects of hijab. Alinejad's rhetoric was similar to the discourse featured in *Tucker Carlson Tonight*, where Carlson sidesteps the positive implications of Macy's pursuit of a hijab fashion line by fixating on hijab as a symptom of the rising Muslim population in the United States and, subsequently, Sharia Law. This fixation plays into femonationalist narratives that demonize Islam while utilizing feminist language that exudes support for the orientalist trope of the oppressed Muslim woman. But *The New York Times* sets itself apart by fully unpacking the economic and social implications that accompany Macy's decision while also recognizing multiple narratives of hijab around the world in various articles. However, apart from *The New York Times*, the overarching discourse across all the news sources was a binary narrative highlighting the hijab as either oppressive or liberating.

Femonationalism: A Not-So Global Sisterhood

Another popular narrative within the news discourse focused on the support, or lack thereof, for Iranian women by American feminists (specifically those affiliated with the Women's March) and hijabi Muslim Americans like Linda Sarsour and U.S. Representative Ilhan Omar. For example, Iranian general Qasem Soleimani was killed on January 3, 2020, after the U.S. launched an airstrike in Baghdad. The strike was ordered by Donald J. Trump's administration, which stated that Soleimani was planning "imminent and sinister attacks on American diplomats and American personnel, but we caught him in the act and terminated him" (Kennedy and Northam, 2020, para 2). Soleimani was a top military leader who led a military organization called the Quds force—a group the United States claims has enabled Iraq to launch attacks on U.S. personnel. Soleimani's death sparked controversy among Americans and Iranians alike, as some categorized his death as an assassination. In a *New York Times* news analysis, David E. Sanger (2020) described the attack as "the riskiest move made by the United States in the Middle East since the invasion on Iraq in 2003." Much of the U.S. Democratic Party disapproved of Trump's attack on Soleimani, including U.S. Representative Ilhan Omar. The dispute was further fueled by debates on whether or not Iran truly mourned the loss of Soleimani or if more Iranians were celebrating his death.

Speaking to that controversy, Alinejad published an article in *The Washington Post* titled, "Don't believe Iranian propaganda about the mourning for Soleimani." Three days after Alinejad expressed vocal support for Soleimani's death, Omar retweeted Eli Clifton, a fellow at *The Nation Institute*, accusing Alinejad of receiving money as a U.S. government contractor and repeatedly giving interviews to *Fox News*. Alinejad appeared on *Fox News' The Story with Martha MacCallum*, exclusively to respond to Omar's retweet. MacCallum (2020) asked Alinejad why Omar was attacking her. She responded:

> I strongly believe that because of my article on "Washington Post." I've criticized Soleimani and I said that many Iranians do not see him as a hero. They see him as a warmonger, as a war criminal. And that is why I got a lot of attacked by the Islamic lobbyist and she actually shared the, one of the defamatory article[s] against me.

Alinejad defends her position as a journalist for *Voice of America* (VOA), a news outlet funded by the U.S. government. But she also uses this media opportunity to confront Omar's lack of support for the women in Iran even after repeated attempts by Alinejad to persuade her to advocate for the #WhiteWednesdays campaign:

> I reached out there a lot. I sent a message to Ilhan Omar, I wrote on Twitter. I wrote an article on "Washington Post" and invited her to join us and show solidarity several times. Once when six women of White Wednesdays got arrested just because of protesting compulsory hijab and other time 29 women in Iran got arrested in one day just because of protesting compulsory hijab. And I asked Ilhan Omar to join us and show solidarity. She was silent. (MacCallum, 2020)

The Washington Post reference mentioned by Alinejad refers to her coauthored article, "There are two types of hijab: The difference is huge." Alinejad and Roya Hakakian (2019) write:

> In an era when nativism is rising in the United States and in many other countries, it is important for those who support the values of a pluralistic society to stand up for the rights of their threatened minorities. In that spirit, we wholeheartedly stand with our Muslim sisters in the West and support their choices. In return, we ask the global sisterhood to stand with Iranian women as they fight against the mandatory hijab.

Alinejad and Hakakian speak to the fear that American feminist support for Iranian women could be framed as Islamophobia, especially when the hijab's normalization in the United States still proves challenging. The authors make a point to directly show support for those Muslim American women with the expectation that Iranian women should receive that same support. Both groups fight against misogyny and discrimination. But the authors unambiguously place a responsibility on Muslim American women to utilize their power and privilege as a platform to advocate for the women of #WhiteWednesdays, explicitly calling out Omar.

Omar and other Muslim women who benefit from the freedom that America has bestowed on them are especially well-positioned to speak up for women forced into hijab.

The authors specifically focus on Omar, as she is a hijabi woman with a position in the U.S. Congress—a hijabi woman in a position of power who has yet to speak on behalf of Iran's women. Omar holds the credibility and authority that Alinejad wants for the #WhiteWednesdays movement and is publishing in a credible, public format (i.e., *The Washington Post*) alongside a credible, Iranian American journalist. The interaction between Alinejad and Omar, as well as *The Washington Post* article, reflects a geopolitical issue in which the tension between the United States and Iran (i.e., Nuclear deal with Iran; sanctions; etc.) influences the problematic lack of support from Western feminists for Iranian women protesters. Alinejad aims to circumvent the issue of Islamophobia by speaking to American feminists on their terms—openly and conspicuously showing support for Muslim American women who choose to wear hijab. However, it is unclear if this is an attempt at transnational feminism or simply a mediated discursive tactic to manipulate American feminists to support the #WhiteWednesdays campaign. Transnational feminism cannot manifest itself when national and political agendas take priority—when it is still an "every *woman* for herself" situation. If geopolitical motives drive feminists, transnational solidarity cannot exist because it transcends the boundaries that geopolitics create.

Alinejad recognizes the political pressure weighing behind the choice of showing support for Iranian women. In the same interview with MacCallum, she says, "Please care about human rights. Human rights should not be lost in the political battles in America." Alinejad's plea speaks to the core issue present in the mainstream news media discourse. Instead of focusing on human rights, the discourse consistently focuses on the politicization of the hijab—a discourse that Alinejad herself contributes to. In another interview with MacCallum, MacCallum asks Alinejad what her message to President Trump is and how America can help the women of #WhiteWednesdays. Alinejad responded with:

Look, I am a woman rights activist. What is important for me is human rights. And Donald Trump actually said he is going to support the people of Iran. First, I want him to remove the Iranian people from the travel ban. (2018)

Alinejad is not concerned with the political complexities within the United States. She repeatedly identifies herself, first and foremost, as a human rights activist; however, identifying as a human rights activist or feminist does not negate one's pursuit of "other political and social goals as well" (Ferree and Tripp, 2006, 7). Human rights have their own political implications as they are often used as a proxy to justify an attack on another country.

The role of American feminists was addressed in another *Fox News* political talk show, *The Five*, in which the anchors criticized the lack of support from American feminists for Iranian women. Greg Gutfeld made claims that American feminists weren't showing support for protesters in Iran because "they're more interested in Obama's false legacy than the actual victims and the brave people out there." He explicitly calls out Linda Sarsour as a "Sharia apologist" who "claims that wearing hijab is some kind of feminist choice when it's by force." The "false legacy" Gutfeld is referring to is the Obama administration's restrained reaction to the 2009 protests in Iran—a significant point of controversy as Obama aimed to limit U.S. involvement in Iranian affairs while human rights violations took place (Tisdall, 2009; Levs, 2012). Gutfield continues:

[American feminists] should be stewing in their own shame for not saying anything about this, for remaining silent, for basically saying that American [o]ppression and Iranian [o]ppression is the same thing. Me Too should be called Them Too, and they should be supporting those women over there [. . .] if you're a feminist and you're talking about the injustice and patriarchy of America and you're not out there defending these women, you're an idiot. (Albano, 2018)

In the same segment, the anchors address American feminists' protests against Islamophobic harassment toward hijabi women in the U.S. American, right-wing conservatives simplify feminist politics to capitalize on the opportunity to promote a femonationalist narrative. The anchors perpetuate an Islamophobic discourse in which they demonize American feminists by underscoring Iranian women's decision to throw off their hijabs—prioritizing the more "serious" issues facing Iranian women while simultaneously demoting American feminism. Furthermore, these anchors use orientalist tropes to their advantage by comparing the plight of Muslim women who appear as "black ghosts by force" to what they call the trivial #MeToo movement in the United States. The construction of feminism perpetuated by the right-wing anchors aligns with their geopolitical ideologies that resist any form of Islamic practices and allows them to discount other American feminists' endeavors such as normalizing the hijab in American culture. *The Five*'s credibility is bolstered by featuring voices from imprisoned Iranian women in another one of the show's segments. The show included the voices of Nasrin Sotoudeh—a prominent human rights lawyer imprisoned for defending multiple women who were arrested for protesting against compulsory hijab—and Sepidoh Gholian—one of the women arrested for protesting against compulsory hijab. In a brief clip, the women were shown speaking with a voice-over translator, saying, "We are the voice of women who are in prison for saying no to forced hijab" (Loker, 2019). While the segment was short, it included something that every other news source did not—except for *CNN*. A segment on *CNN* also featured women's voices on the ground, showing an extended clip of Iranian women being harassed by Iran's morality police for wearing inappropriate hijab (Abdelaziz, 2019). The clip was provided and narrated by Alinejad.

In another episode of *Tucker Carlson Tonight*, Carlson invites Zuhdi Jasser, president of the American Islamic Forum for Democracy, to discuss the 2019 *Sports Illustrated Swimsuit Edition* featuring a model wearing both hijab and a burqini. Jasser responded to American feminists as well as NBC's *The Today Show*'s support of the magazine's feature:

> Let's look at the left's attitude about this. I thought they were the ones about women's rights and equality and not objectifying women? And the #MeToo folks, so how does this use of the hijab and the burqini in which it's used to torture women in Iran and Saudi Arabia, if they don't wear it, if they don't comply; it's a symbol of actual oppression.
>
> Now somehow the "Today" show folks think this is a symbol of equality and expression, I mean it really is irrational no matter which way you look at it. (Wells, 2019)

The producers at *Fox News* enable a discursive strategy by utilizing the voice of an elite source and Muslim advocate—the president of an organization that "addresses the root cause of Islamist radicalization" and focuses on the assimilation of immigrant Muslim communities to American lifestyles (aifdemocracy.org). In the interview, Jasser supports orientalist stereotypes and femonationalist rhetoric by arguing for one single dimension of hijab—oppression—while subsequently ignoring the Islamophobic issues that reside in the United States. Strategically, Jasser uses feminist language to diminish the hijab, especially in the United States, and supposedly defend oppressed Muslim women. Jasser, a Muslim American man, is attempting to speak with authority on an issue affecting Muslim women—an experience he cannot have as a Muslim man. Yet, no woman, Iranian or not, is present to speak to what is clearly a woman's issue. Instead, a patriarchal, orientalist discourse is mediated through a right-wing news source, strategically depicting Carlson and Jasser as advocates rather than femonationalists.

Carlson continues his femonationalist narrative in his interview with the head of the New York branch of NOW, Sonia Ossorio, to discuss Macy's decision to sell hijabs.

> *Carlson:* I mean the point of Islamic clothing is to promote modesty among women for a bunch of reasons. It's in the Quran. It's, of course, a central part of Islamic culture. So, are you for that? Do you think women should be coerced to dress modestly? Is that a feminist goal?
>
> *Ossorio:* I think what a feminist goal is, is for women to be in control of their lives and their destinies and to have choices. So, whether a woman wants to wear a hijab or she doesn't is really not the point.
>
> *Carlson:* Wait, wait. I'm confused. It's not the point. So, if I say as Islamic countries, you don't have a choice, you have to wear hijab because you need to be modest. And if you are not, you could get raped. And if you do, it's your fault. And if you have to avert your gaze from men and touch non-relatives who are men. Is that OK with you? (Wells, 2018)

Carlson references Chinese foot-binding and female genital mutilation when asking Ossario how practices deemed oppressive in some contexts may empower others. Despite Ossario's attempts to describe the shifting meanings of hijab depending on place and context, an essential aspect of transnational feminism, Carlson continues to criticize Ossario's logic that the hijab can be both empowering and oppressive. Carlson supports women forced to wear hijab by condemning the normalization of hijab in American department stores and comparing the head covering to Chinese foot-binding and female genital mutilation. In this way, he promotes femonationalist rhetoric by equating the practice of hijab in the United States with those women in Iran forced to wear hijab—which negates the individual lived experiences of hijabi women. Furthermore, he uses Ossario, theoretically a credible feminist source, to prove his point while simultaneously mocking American feminists working to eradicate Islamophobia in the United States.

Amid the critiques of American feminists and binary arguments on the hijab, one article distinctly shifted away from callout culture. Nazanin Boniadi (2018), an Iranian American actress, wrote an online article for *CNN* saying:

While I was encouraged by the numerous signs supporting women, I was disheartened that in this time of female solidarity we were largely ignorant of our counterparts in Iran, who just weeks prior to our march had risked arrest or worse to take to the streets and demand their inalienable rights.

Boniadi does not shy away from her convictions and instead shares them with her contemporary American feminists by juxtaposing the 2018 Women's March with the #WhiteWednesdays campaign in Iran. She admits that the true practice of "female solidarity" includes recognizing women fighting different battles in other parts of the world—specifically, Iranian women. Later in the article, she writes:

> The timing of the Women's Marches and the women protesting in Iran are not a coincidence, but a convergence. These episodes are part of a global awakening in women's rights, and these expressions of bravery and civil disobedience must not be viewed as isolated incidents—even if they are not organized under one banner.

Boniadi does not describe the timing of the protests as serendipitous or a matter of happenstance. Instead, she illustrates these events as "a global awakening in women's rights." Boniadi is expressing the essence of transnational feminism—the practice of working toward women's rights within shifting cultural, political, and geographical contexts—by broadening the definition of feminism in acknowledging the shifting struggles and forms of protest across international borders. Boniadi also recognizes the tendency to categorize these events as separate actions when, at the core, they are the same. Boniadi is responding to the call Alinejad is making to women like Sarsour and Omar, who err on the side of protecting against Islamophobic rhetoric as well as standing with particular political stances. In this way, Boniadi utilizes her privilege to speak directly to American feminists on behalf of Iranian women, building a bridge that transcends borders.

THE SHIFTING ROLE OF IRANIAN WOMEN: FROM VICTIM TO WARRIOR

Across all of the news outlets, journalists and sources characterized Iranian women using language that depicted them as warriors instead of stereotypical frames often used by journalists in the past (Mishra, 2007; Terman, 2017; Kumar, 2018). The mainstream news discourse surrounding #WhiteWednesdays described Iranian women as "brave," "strong," and "defiant." In an interview with *Fox News* television host Martha MacCallum,

Alinejad elaborated on the fearlessness of Iranian women protesting on the ground:

> I'm not hopeless because every individual woman they became their own, you know, leader. They are not waiting for anyone to come and save them, to come and rescue them. They are the warriors instead of being like a victim. (2018)

Additionally, Alinejad routinely communicates the perseverance of the #WhiteWednesdays movement despite the increasing number of arrests of women protesters. For example, in Alinejad's (2019) article, "My Brother Ali is Iran's Latest Hostage," published in *The Wall Street Journal*, she writes:

> In August, six women were sentenced to a combined 109 years for peacefully protesting the compulsory hijab [. . .] If the authorities thought this would scare off Iranian women, they were wrong. Women continue to send me videos of their resistance.

Fox News also highlighted the fierce nature of Alinejad. For example, before segueing into an interview with Alinejad, *The Story with Martha MacCallum* included an excerpt from her speech at the 2016 Women in the World New York Summit:

> So, we, the women of Iran breaking the laws every day to just be ourselves. And I'm a master criminal, why? Because the government of Iran thinks I have too much hair, I have too much voice and I am too much of a woman. (2018)

Additionally, Alinejad often featured her own fearlessness with quotes like the following:

> We are challenging one of the main pillars of the Islamic. That is why actually they are really scared of us and the campaign that I, you know, have in Iran and that is why they brought my family in Iranian TV to disown me publicly . . . Rich men especially the Islamic republic officials they are really scared of strong women, and now women in Iran they are leading the movement. The movement [is] gaining momentum. (MacCallum, 2018)

Alinejad highlights a shifting power dynamic from the Islamic Republic to the women of Iran. She describes herself as "too much of a woman" in a way that implies a dangerous nature—at least as far as her "womanness" poses a threat to the Iranian government. Alinejad continues to perpetuate this narrative saying, "they are really scared of us . . . they are really scared of strong women, and now women in Iran are leading the movement." The language used here illustrates an illumination of the power Iranian women hold and the support they require to maintain that power.

However, when Alinejad speaks of Iranian women, she often references herself. In many of the examples above, she homogenizes Iranian women using characteristics she uses to describe herself. She allows her voice to be elevated by the news media by literally presenting herself as the Iranian woman's struggle personified—a problematic tactic that promotes a singular view of the events happening on the ground. Consequently, the audience's gaze is fixed on Alinejad's image without an option to look to anyone else because the sources included in the coverage are limited. There is no outlet to check her representation or the interests she serves (della Porta and Tarrow, 2004), as mainstream news coverage of Alinejad is increasingly homogenous (Fenton, 2015).

Shifting away from singing the praises of Alinejad, *The New York Times* featured an article on the conviction of prominent Iranian human rights lawyer Nasrin Sotoudeh. Sotoudeh is known for defending many Iranian women who were jailed for defying compulsory hijab—a job that eventually led to her arrest. In the article, Gladstone (2019) calls her "an international symbol of defiance to the limits on personal and political freedoms imposed by the Islamic Republic's religious hierarchy." While the language used to describe Sotoudeh's arrest highlights her bravery, it also uses her actions as a way to target the Islamic Republic through the violation of human rights.

While these so-called empowering descriptions were plentiful in the news discourse, orientalist stereotypes were not wholly absent. A *USA Today* article, "In Iran, most women must live as second-class citizens, but some are making strides," contained some of the victimizing language routinely used in news discourse to describe women living under an Islamic regime. Hjelmgaard (2018) opens her article with a vignette of nineteen-year-old Kimia Naderzadeh, who "is not interested in testing the limits of laws that clearly treat her as vastly inferior to a man." She continues:

> Like millions of other Islamic women in Iran, Naderzadeh, a makeup artist and model, grudgingly accepts she must follow strict rules that dictate how she lives her life, down to the clothing she can wear in public.

Hjelmgaard (2018) sets the stage with a verbal image of an apathetic Iranian woman taking no action to change her status as a "second-class citizen" or showing solidarity with the women who do. She refers to "millions of other Islamic women in Iran" and implies that the Iranian women resisting the regime are the exception rather than the rule. The article's introductory paragraphs fall into orientalist narratives that illustrate Muslim women in passive roles that inevitably victimize them (Terman, 2017). Additionally,

Hjelmgaard (2018) goes on to idealize the pre-1979 era—a time when the United States and Iran were on good terms—without any mention of the country's restrictions on women at that time, such as the banning of the veil. Instead, she focuses on the Western clothing Iranian women were wearing before the revolution:

> Miniskirts, shorts, tight jeans and even bikinis were once highly fashionable for women in Iran under the last monarch nearly four decades ago. Yet since the founding of the Islamic Republic in 1979, women's rights have been severely circumscribed, including how they choose to dress. (August 29, 2018)

Hjelmgaard (2018) strategically juxtaposes the Iranian woman's fashion experience pre-1979 with the rules of fashion post-1979 as a way to illustrate what life used to be like—when the United States and Iran were on good terms, and Iran served as a lucrative benefit to the United States.

While Hjelmgaard (2018) conveniently does not address the women's rights issues pre-1979, she does spend the second half of her article highlighting the defiance of some women working to improve the status of women's rights in Iran in a sub-section titled, "Not passive in the face of inequality." She interviews an Iranian woman, who serves as a media consultant for a news service in London, on the subject:

> Women have been able to push for greater representation in the workforce and in politics, and in Iran's cultural and social fabric more generally. A lot of (women's rights) activists will say that things are going slower than they hoped, but they have been very persistent and that deserves to be recognized.

Again, while Hjelmgaard (2018) opens her article with orientalist tropes of Muslim women, she shifts from victimizing language to illustrations of Iranian women practicing agency over their circumstances. Hjelmgaard's (2018) structure could either be strategic or problematic (or both), depending on if the audience goes beyond the first half of the article. If not, Hjelmgaard's (2018) piece falls into the pile of stereotypical news pieces featuring Muslim women. Nevertheless, Hjelmgaard's (2018) shift from victim to agent fits with her pre-1979 narrative when women's rights allowed for miniskirts, tight jeans, and bikinis or, in other words, Western fashion. The shift here emphasizes the opportunity to revert to the "good ole days," which also coincides with the U.S. geopolitical agenda pushing for regime change in Iran. News media discourse here implies that life was better for women when the Shah was in power, when Iran enjoyed the Era of Modernization (otherwise known as westernization), and the United States benefited from its strategic relationship with the Shah. Furthermore, by maintaining the focus on women's rights, the narrative is disguised as the United States operating with altruistic motives. But the underlying mediated message here underscores the historical relationship between the United States and Iran while elevating the notion that women's rights is an ideal entry point to facilitate U.S. intervention.

In sum, the majority of the news coverage presented a binary narrative of hijab, giving audiences a limited understanding of the issues facing women involved in the #WhiteWednesdays campaign. Furthermore, the discourse focused heavily on the hijab itself instead of the core issue of Muslim women's right to choose. Reporters from at least three news sources (*CNN, Fox News*, and *The New York Times*) used the Macy's story to make a spectacle of the hijab and the #WhiteWednesdays campaign. However, *CNN* and *Fox News* overlooked women's voices on the ground and instead relied on elite news sources with well-known reputations.

Additionally, given the silence on the part of American Muslim women, *Fox News* was able to capitalize on the lack of advocacy from American feminists to promote femonationalist rhetoric laden with support for Iranian women and disdain for the hijab and other Islamic practices infiltrating the United States. *The Washington Post* featured two news stories written by Alinejad, lending the activist a platform to make her own judgments on American feminists, alongside noted Iranian American journalist Roya Hakakian, who also enhanced Alinejad's discourse with a sense of credibility and authority as well as a chance to shape the narrative on #WhiteWednesdays. Part of Alinejad's narrative centered on her own bravery, strength, and initiative to lead an overthrow of the Iranian patriarchy with the help of her Western counterpart, and current homeland, the United States. Overall, news media reflected the West's obsession with the veil to promote the #WhiteWednesdays campaign by elevating Alinejad's voice and discourse on the hijab. The hyper-focus on Alinejad deterred the discourse from a transnational perspective and instead prompted a femonationalist rhetoric demonizing hijab, Iran, and American Muslim feminists.

Finally, news discourse showed support for the women of #WhiteWednesdays by incorporating Alinejad's descriptions of the women as brave, persistent warriors fighting against the Islamic Republic's ideology. By consistently highlighting Alinejad's discourse on Iranian women's battle against the "pillars of Islam," "the government of Iran," and the "Islamic Republic," the news discourse employed a strategy used to idealize the pre-1979 era when women were free to be "modern" (i.e., Western). Furthermore, by focusing on women's rights before and after the Islamic revolution, the news discourse elevated women's rights to promote U.S. intervention—reminiscent of the Era of Modernization when the United States and Iran were geopolitical allies.

Chapter 7

Twitter Analysis

The Twitter discourse analyzed in this study highlighted issues of representation, including debates on transnational feminist politics and critiques of Western feminists' expressions of solidarity with Muslim women. However, the primary difference between the Twitter discourse and the news discourse was the population of diverse voices from Iranian women on the ground. Social movements have often turned to social media as a space for alternative discourse controlled by the news cycle's gatekeepers. Alternative-activist new media allows for a different narrative structure that highlights context and a more bottom-up discursive approach underscoring the basis of the movement (Harlow and Johnson, 2011; Fenton, 2016).

Based on the number of tweets dedicated to challenging Alinejad's self-proclaimed role as a representative of Iranian women, one of the most prevalent contention points was the debate on transnational feminist politics. Iranians employed Twitter to hold Alinejad's public discourse and actions to account, following her media timeline and judging her appearances accordingly. While a consensus was never reached on Alinejad's credibility as a representative of Iranian women, the conversation remained dynamic as protesters recognized when their rights and interests were and were not acknowledged. Additionally, Twitter served as a space to challenge the Muslim woman's traditional archetype by critiquing Western feminists' expressions of solidarity with Muslim women—manifestations that often mirrored orientalist tropes by exaggerating the role of hijab. Furthermore, Iranian feminists used Twitter as a public forum to debate and promote specific forms of solidarity. These debates frequently included negating the actions of public figures like Linda Sarsour, a Palestinian-American activist and cochair of the U.S. Women's March, and U.S. Representative Ilhan Omar. But this discourse did not always challenge news discourses and, in some cases, reaffirmed them instead. Overall, the Twitter discourse revealed a tension between transnational feminism and femonationalism as well as the continued perpetuation of a binary narrative on hijab—similar to the narrative bolstered by the majority of news discourse examined in the previous chapter.

CONTESTING AND CONSTRUCTING TRANSNATIONAL FEMINIST POLITICS

While Alinejad did not necessarily control the Twitter discourse, she appeared to dictate the conversations online and offline. Alinejad's role as an activist was consistently up for debate, likely due to her "framing power" (Carvalho, 2008) as both a journalist and an Iranian source for the protests occurring on the ground. The controversy surrounding Alinejad dealt heavily with her assumed duty as a representative of Iranian women and, at times, the Iranian people as a whole. The discourse concerning Alinejad's role emerged as a debate on whether or not Alinejad sufficiently represented Iranian women's voices. The dispute regarding Alinejad's authentic representation escalated after Alinejad made a Twitter announcement about her official meeting with U.S. Secretary of State Mike Pompeo to discuss the #WhiteWednesdays campaign. Some Iranians responded with excitement:

@Nazaninmrzn: @AlinejadMasih and @SecPompeo It was definitely the best news these days. Masih [*sic*] has always been and still is the voice of the people. This is like meeting the Iranian people with Mike Pompeo. (Nazanin, 2019)

@care4brain: @AlinejadMasih and @SecPompeo What a great news. Iran needs a regime change and we need more support from the rest of the world. And you . . . are truley an amazing messanger. As an iranian woman i am always proud of you. We dream together about a free Iran! (2019)

Above, Alinejad is regarded as a representative not only of Iranian women but of Iran itself. She is meeting with an American dignitary, which, as one user put it, is like the Iranian people themselves meeting with Pompeo. Alinejad also received validation from an Iranian woman who calls her "an amazing messenger" and subsequently supports Alinejad's efforts to garner international assistance—even with a country responsible for the sanctions on Iran. Tweets like those above enhance Alinejad's credibility as a representative, likely because these Twitter users believe Alinejad is working on their behalf. But, given the problematic politics of representation, tweets of frustration and disapproval far outweighed those of support for Alinejad's meeting with Pompeo. For example:

@Goldenwheatsami: It's none of your business/You aren't my voice and my nation's voice/So plz be silence. (2019)

@mitrabahri: @Alinejadmasih and @SecPompeo How could you dare even imagining that you are the voice of Iranian people when they are under the worst sanction dictated by the very person who you are officially meeting with?!?! (Bahri, 2019)

@AmirMohamad474: Iranian women have been oppressed for so long, and they deserve a voice, however it's unfortunate that you have been the poster child for this movement, when I see you, I see a person who have made a career out of being a rebel, I see someone whose ultimate goal is not freedom for . . . (2019—account suspended)

The tweets above highlight the problematic nature of Alinejad's meeting (as an un-elected, self-proclaimed representative of Iran) with the U.S. Secretary of State—mainly because of the United States' withdrawal from the Nuclear Deal in 2019—which resulted in the reinstatement of sanctions placed on Iran and, therefore, further crippling the country's economy (Gelvin, 2017; U.S. Virtual Embassy of Iran, 2019). Because Pompeo was a significant player in this decision-making process, some Iranians see Alinejad as an opportunistic activist looking for her 15 minutes of fame. These Iranian Twitter users acknowledge Alinejad's problematic framing power as one user calls her "the poster child for this movement." These Iranians are seeking to highlight her lack of credibility to separate themselves from her discourse broadcasted on American television. Iranian women "deserve a voice," but the nature of the #WhiteWednesdays campaign's representation presents the issue that instead of promoting women's rights in Iran, Alinejad is promoting certain rights for certain women in Iran. Alinejad's message strategically appeals to particular political actors to ensure her end goal—U.S. support for her campaign (Hawkesworth, 2006).

Alinejad's actions and discourse stimulated conversation among Iranians who took to Twitter to challenge her broadcasted narratives and fight for their right to be heard instead of relying on Alinejad's representation. Social movements like #WhiteWednesdays often turn to social media to promote their campaigns to reach both policymakers and the public as a whole (Hermida, 2010; Harlow and Johnson, 2011). Protesters recognize that social media is a way to bypass gatekeepers that routinely call on elite sources to shape the social movement's narrative, rather than the protesters themselves (Hermida et al., 2014). Additionally, social media platforms allow for a different narrative structure typically used by mainstream news sources. This alternative structure recognizes more in-depth and contextualized information, more alternative voices, and more grassroots participation—a key element in alternative-activist new media (Harlow and Johnson, 2011; Fenton, 2016; Mislán and Dache-Gerbino, 2018). The counter-publics created on Twitter provide an opportunity for a bottom-up discursive approach that is often neglected in mainstream news, leading to a skewed storyline based on privileged voices. But, protesters' use of Twitter allows them to shape the narrative and hold their representatives (elected or not) to account, much like the Twitter users do here with Alinejad.

Alinejad received similar pushback after testifying before the Canadian Foreign Affairs Committee in May 2019, again on behalf of the women of #WhiteWednesdays:

> Hmg60671352: @AlinejadMasih Why do you think you can talk on behalf of Iranian people? Just because of the number of your followers? You can just talk on behalf of people who pay you. Shame on you. (2019)

In each of the examples, there is an emphasis on "voice," likely due to the recognition of Alinejad's framing power and her access to Western leaders and journalists. Iranians are highlighting the flawed testament Alinejad presents in powerful spaces that can affect Iran as a whole, with the help of other influential actors looking to isolate Iran and promote regime change. The danger of a single story is prevalent here because Alinejad's testimony can have geopolitical consequences—much like the sanctions on Iran weakening the economy and, subsequently, the people.

Iranian women on Twitter continued to challenge Alinejad's rhetoric after she posted two *Vogue* magazine photos—one of them exposing her hair titled, "Meet the Iconoclast Inspiring Iranian Women to Remove Their Headscarves," and the other of Ilhan Omar clad in hijab titled, "Ilhan Omar: 'To me, the Hijab Means Power, Liberation, Beauty, and Resistance.'" She writes:

> When I appeared in Vogue some leftists attacked & said anti compulsory hijab campaigner can't be in a capitalist fashion magazine. Now they praise @Ilhan. How hypocritical. They have no problem if Vogue is pro hijab. To me fighting compulsory hijab means power beauty & resistance. (2019)

Again, Alinejad is projecting a binary narrative on the hijab while creating an "us vs. them" framework between her and Omar—two women with distinctly different views on hijab—or Muslim women in the global South versus Muslim women in the global North. But, while Alinejad negated the substance of transnational feminism, Iranian women did not.

@sham_marral: No, Vogue is pro-women's choice @AlinejadMasih. Your Islamophobic feminism cosies up to the far-right, denies hijabi women agency, and targets innocent women whose resistance and feminism far exceeds yours. (Marral, 2019)

She continues in a separate tweet:

@sham_marral: The anti-compulsory hijab movement is important in Iran. But to suggest that hijabi women in the West (or even MENA) submit to oppression on choosing hijab is wrong and only alienates Muslim women. #WhiteWednesdays is resistance, but Islamophobic far-right backed feminism sucks. (2019)

@sham_marral's tweets speak directly to the nature of transnational feminism by rebuking Alinejad's rhetoric that fuels what @sham_marral calls "Islamophobic far-right backed feminism." @sham_marral senses the femonationalist aspects of Alinejad's discourse and unambiguously calls her out. The response also challenges Alinejad's practice of resistance and feminism by implying a hierarchy of feminism and a misrepresentation of feminism in general. @sham_marral accuses Alinejad of denying "hijab women agency" and targeting "innocent women"—it can be assumed that she is referring to Omar—possibly suggesting that one cannot promote feminism while simultaneously tearing other women down—the antithesis of transnational feminism. This idea of competing ideologies reflects the complexity of transnational feminism by underscoring its fluid nature and its decentralization of power. While no panel or committee exists to validate or invalidate one's feminist actions, feminists recognize that feminism is not an arbitrary concept. That recognition fuels the practice of transnational feminism as seen on Twitter, where Iranian feminists publicly disagreed and reflected on the nuances in feminist activism while also attempting to neutralize feminism's global hegemony (Hawkesworth, 2006).

In other Twitter posts, users continued to operate within this transnational feminist paradigm to counteract Alinejad's single narrative of feminism. A similar case was illustrated after Alinejad promoted her interview with an Italian magazine about her thoughts on Italian High Representative of the Union for Foreign Affairs and Security Policy and the EU's foreign policy chief, Federica Mogherini.

@AlinejadMasih: I'm giving an interview to an #Italian magazine about Federica Mogherini who betrayed #Iranian people, especially #women, for the sake of the nuclear deal which only benefited the regime. @FedericaMog (2018)

The tweet was accompanied by a photo of Mogherini wearing a hijab and shaking hands with Iranian prime minister Mohammad Javad Zarif. In this tweet, Alinejad is taking a similar position on the Nuclear Deal as the United States—ironic given the economic sanctions placed on Iran following the withdrawal of the United States from the Nuclear Deal. Because Alinejad is an Iranian woman activist, her disregard for the Nuclear Deal helps to validate the U.S. decision to abandon the deal—a choice that sparked much controversy against the United States and the Trump administration. However, men and women activists from Iran did not allow Alinejad to have the final word in this case:

> @mehrza: @AlinejadMasih and @FedericaMog Maybe you should first tell that "Italian" magazine how you managed to become a (paid to play) "activist" all of a sudden AFTER keeping your hair covered even after you were living outside of Iran for more than 2 years! You are nothing but a #propaganda_tool for #WarProfiteers. (Mehrzad, 2018)

In the tweet above, @mehrza refers to Alinejad's choice to continue covering her hair with a cap even after leaving Iran because she felt uncomfortable—she notes this in her book *The Wind in My Hair*. This is worth noting because Alinejad is adamantly against the practice of hijab yet did not feel comfortable uncovering her hair for two years after leaving Iran. Also, @mehrza calls Alinejad a "paid to play" activist. This refers to her payment from the U.S. State Department of more than $230,000 for "her commentary and anti-compulsory hijab activism in Iran" (Harvard, 2018). @Mehrza also calls Alinejad a propaganda tool—a reference to her meetings with U.S. Secretary of State Mike Pompeo, who she met with during the Trump administration's campaign to isolate Iran (Moaveni, 2018).

> @Tamaashaaa: @AlinejadMasih @kargadan and @FedericaMog Would you please stop advocating for the people you yourself betrayed at the first place? We know the organizations that fund your activity. You might think you are a hero, you might love the idea of being a hero. But you are just a puppet. (Tamasha, 2018)

> @khamiaze: @AlinejadMasih and @FedericaMog Consider giving an interview to an #Italian magazine about Masih Alinejad who betrays #Iranian people, men and #women, by standing alongside Trump and Iranian hardliners for the sake of the cheap attention she begs for. @FedericaMog (2018)

In the two tweets above, Twitter users accuse Alinejad of betraying the Iranian people—meaning she started as a genuine activist working exclusively on behalf of Iranian women but has since used her U.S. government connections to gain both money and fame. Again, the Iranian Twitter users make it clear that Alinejad's betrayal lies within her relationship with Trump and Pompeo because of their choice to instill economic sanctions on Iran—theoretically on behalf of the people (Moaveni, 2018). As a result of Alinejad's relationship with the Trump administration, her rhetoric becomes a tool to work on behalf of the Trump administration's geopolitical agenda to continue isolating Iran by highlighting the regime's human rights violations. Consequently, while alternative discourses exist on social media, their reach is only possible when a privileged voice is amplified (Fenton, 2015). In this case, #WhiteWednesdays is heavily dependent on Alinejad as thousands of women entrusted her with their photos and videos—enhancing her framing power. As Fenton (2015) argues, "strong, popular, widespread, even global protest can be and frequently is entirely ignored by the powerful" (p. 355).

CONSTITUTING AND NEGATING
EXPRESSIONS OF SOLIDARITY

The symbol of the hijab has become an archetype for Muslim women. Thus, the donning of the hijab has evolved into a popular way of showing solidarity with Muslim women (Azadi, 2015). Some researchers find this problematic, mainly because of the reductionist view of Muslim women that excludes their global diversity (Yuval-Davis, 2015; Gokarksel and Smith, 2017; Rahbari, 2019). For instance, Yuval-Davis (2015) argues that due to the West's infatuation with the veil (Abu-Lughod, 2013), Muslim women's intersectionality has been ignored. Instead, the hijab has become a part of the hegemonic imagery associated with Muslim women—imagery that overlooks Muslim women who do not wear hijab. This hegemonic interpretation is continuously perpetuated through campaigns focused on solidarity with Muslim women like World Hijab Day—a campaign encouraging non-Muslim women to wear hijab for a day to better understand the dangerous lived experience of Muslim women (WorldHijabDay.com). However, when non-Muslim women choose to wear hijab as an act of solidarity, they are only performing solidarity with a) Muslim women who wear hijab; and b) Muslim women in the West facing Islamophobia. Other Muslim women's lived experiences with hijab are neglected (Rahbari, 2019; Rahbari et al., 2019).

In the #WhiteWednesdays Twitter discourse, a debate on the constitution of solidarity emerged—specifically related to the hijab. For example, Alinejad posted a news article titled "New Zealand women face praise and protests for donning the hijab," published after the Christchurch mosque shooting. She tweeted:

Now I call on New Zealand women to show their sisterhood and solidarity with us, who are being beaten up, imprisoned and punished for fighting against compulsory hijab as well. Masih Alinejad told Reuters. #WhiteWednesdays (2019)

Alinejad is petitioning for the same Western women who defended victims of Islamophobia to show the same support for the women of #WhiteWednesdays—similar to Sarsour's call for Iranian women to support Muslim American women vulnerable to Islamophobia. Alinejad is challenging the Muslim woman's hegemonic imagery by highlighting the lived experiences of Muslim women forced to wear hijab. Some Iranians communicated convictions similar to Alinejad:

> @sharshalimar: Visit Iran as true sisters and start a real protest by taking off your head scarf THEN YOU SHOW SOLIDARITY WITH MUSLIM WOMEN!!!

> Wearing a headscarf for fun in a free country, indeed start fighting for your sisters who haven't got that freedom and show true solidarity. (Farahdi, 2019)

The tweet above showcases the academic theorization surrounding the constitution of solidarity. @sharshalimar criticizes the women in New Zealand for wearing an Islamic symbol they do not identify with "for fun" and a negation of "true solidarity" by using language targeting feminists with the use of "sisters." Additionally, @sharshalimar's rebuke of the New Zealand women also suggests a homogenization of Muslim women's experience with hijab—even those living within Iran. She uses Twitter to write with the authority to speak on behalf of all Muslim women as well as the constitution of solidarity. Other Twitter users also expressed disapproval of the way Westerners show solidarity with Muslim women:

> @MoradiAskar: The duplicity of Western politicians is well known, it has nothing to do with human rights and freedom. To do it for their own economic gain. (Askar, 2019)

@MoradiAskar's tweet speaks directly to Barnett and Land's (2007) "geographies of generosity"—when "caring from afar" enables the ability to show partiality with a cause one does not necessarily identify with but could receive benefits. In this case, @MoradiAskar claims that Western politician's goals are not altogether altruistic, having nothing to do with human rights, but rather self-serving in terms of economic gain. The women of #WhiteWednesdays would serve as political pawns for the other Western nations to further their own geopolitical agendas. However, while the tweets from @sharshalimar and @MoradiAskar appear defensive on behalf of

Iranian women, they are also akin to the femonationalist arguments made by Western, right-wing conservatives by explicitly defining what "a real protest" looks like or specifying a singular manifestation of solidarity with Muslim women. This constitution of Muslim solidarity implies that Western women must support the eradication of compulsory hijab in Iran by negating hijab altogether, regardless of context—a sharp shift away from transnational feminism that privileges context.

In addition to the criticism aimed at the women in New Zealand, there was one notable exception within the Twitter discourse:

> @golrizgozari: Nonsense !!!!!!!!! With this card you have a lot to question. The prime minister of New Zealand actually displayed a form of sympathy and respect for Muslims. At the same time, with the intelligence and anthropology and sociology that he knows, they are part of the vengeful community and part of their Jihad. (Gozari, 2019)

Twitter user @golrizgozari challenges Alinejad's constitution of solidarity with Muslim women and appeals to a form of solidarity advocated by Featherstone (2012) in which solidarity does not require a foundation of similarity, only a willingness to challenge hegemonic forces of oppression. However, a problematic interpretation of solidarity remains. Those advocating for New Zealand's literal materialization of solidarity with Muslim women ignore those women's problematic composition. Representing solidarity with Muslim women following the Christchurch mosque shooting in this way invalidates those women who practice Islam but do not wear hijab—those women that are not "visibly Muslim." Therefore, the perpetuation of a singular characterization of Muslim women continues to circulate and reinforce stereotypical illustrations.

Throughout the Twitter discourse, Alinejad continued to promote a specific form of solidarity that homogenizes Iranian women's lived experiences with the hijab. For example, following Belgian ambassador Veronique Petite's choice to make a diplomatic trip to Iran and comply with compulsory hijab, Alinejad reprimanded the ambassador's actions and accused her of aiding the Islamic Republic's retention of power:

> I call on Belgian and other Western news outlets as well as all feminists in the world to condemn the fact that Veronique Petite legitimized discriminatory law by obeying it. This is how they're helping the Islamic Republic put further pressure on Iranian women. (2019)

Alinejad's tweet presents a question of responsibility and priority in terms of human rights, which Iranians debated on Twitter. Some users sided with

Alinejad and claimed that it would have been better for the ambassador to have stayed at home:

> @MFarahani: The ambassador should be ashamed of this appearance. Very sad. (Farahani, 2019)

> @itsmeafshin: Ambassador Petite; you may please a few percentage of occupier of our country but let me say, you are an obstructive to freedom and women's emancipation. Let IRI comes to your country, or let your country sends a male rep to Iran Do Not support murderers, corrupts and abusers. (Afshin, 2019)

However, other Iranian Twitter users expressed a need for compromise due to the economic sanctions placed on Iran:

> @ninianomada: These ambassadors may provide support to shipment of health equipment and basic needs items to respond to flood emergency in Iran for women and children while regular shipping is restricted due to the sanctions, the sanctions which we know whom are the supporters. (2019)

The tweet above underscores the question of the lesser evil—should the ambassador (a) refuse to meet with Iran under the circumstances of compulsory hijab and compromise aid for Iranians; or (b) advocate for human rights by compromising her support for #WhiteWednesdays to ensure that the Iranian people are receiving the aid they need. The overarching question is, can the ambassador support #WhiteWednesdays while ensuring the safety of Iranians? This is a critical inquiry that should be highlighted by Iranian people on the ground rather than journalists without any stake in the game.

In addition to the criticism against Alinejad and Petite, Linda Sarsour's lack of support for #WhiteWednesdays also presented a point of contention within the Twitter discourse. Sarsour became one of the Women's March national cochairs in 2018, shortly after the #WhiteWednesdays campaign launched. On the eve of the Women's March, Alinejad tweeted her intention to participate in the march in hopes of elevating the Iranian women's campaign to end compulsory hijab. Sarsour had yet to show any public support for the #WhiteWednesdays campaign and already had a reputation for being a Sharia law supporter, both within the United States and abroad in Iran. Iranians and Iranian Americans did not take to Alinejad's participation kindly because of Sarsour's heavy involvement with the protest. In response, they created the hashtag #BackOffLinda to send the message that they did not need or desire her support:

> @NilooGholami: Iranian women and Iranian feminists are NOT on the SAME SIDE with Islam apologists like @lsarsour. Islam and Sharia law are the cause

of all misery Iranian women have been through, so #BackOffLinda. (Gholami, 2018)

@meynooshh: You are #fake_ feminist and sinister muslim. In Iran women are aware and know you and Islamic terrorism. #BackOffLinda. (Meynoosh, 2018)

@atosa24: @lsarsour Shut up Linda! We Iranian women know too well what "real Islam" is! We also know too well who is paying you to promote sharia law! You can fool clueless Westerners, but we have experienced up close what Islam does to women! #BackOffLinda. (Atosa, 2018)

Iranian women protesting on the ground are adamantly against everything Sarsour stands for; therefore, they do not want her name associated with their campaign even if Alinejad is petitioning for her support—as was apparent in her interviews on *CNN* and *Fox News*, as well as her articles in *The Washington Post*. Iranian women are responding to Alinejad by proclaiming that she does not speak for them exclusively, and they will not accept Sarsour as an ally based on Alinejad's discretion. On the other hand, some women recognized the alt-right's attempts to appropriate #WhiteWednesdays for their own political goals, including the discrediting Sarsour, and came to her defense:

@mathcolorstress: I'm an Iranian-American Feminist and against the forced Hijab in Iran and I support @lsarsour. The Women's March and Iranian feminists are on the SAME SIDE, both defending women's choice and autonomy. The alt-right can not appropriate our mutual struggle for freedom. (Roja, 2017)

The above tweet was accompanied by a meme published by an alt-right political commentator, Jack Posobiec, showing Sarsour's photo next to Movahed holding her white hijab on the end of a stick. Sarsour's photo was labeled "Fake Feminist," while Movahed's was labeled "Real Feminist," followed by the caption "Choose Wisely." Nevertheless, the tweet from @mathcolorstress was met with backlash like the following:

@Dora_kula: I'm an Iranian feminist and I don't support @lsarsour who says hijab empowers women. This is dangerously distorted from the truth. It reminds me of the Mullahs who've being twisted words like this for 40 years. What empowers women is having choice. #BackOffLinda. (den Drömmare, 2018)

The tweets above showcase a public discourse on Sarsour's role as a feminist and a representative of American Muslim women. By openly disagreeing and recognizing multiple points of view of Muslim women, feminism, and hijab, these feminist activists are modeling what Hawkesworth (2006) calls "a different mode of democratic practice as they struggle against global hegemony" (p. 145). But, while the democratic practice is apparent, the remaining issue lies in the absence of another pivotal aspect of transnational feminism—comparing different forms of oppression without creating a hierarchy of oppression or trying to establish a unified definition of that oppression (Grewal and Kaplan, 1994). Therefore, if the women involved in the discourse cannot express respect for political, cultural, and geographical context and nuance, this discourse cannot be described as a form of transnational feminism. Furthermore, if the tweet above demonstrates an indifference to @mathcolorstress' claim that the alt-right is capitalizing on the #WhiteWednesdays campaign, then there is no concern for the global North's appropriation of women's movements in the global South. On the contrary, among all of the #BackkOffLinda tweets, it appears that Iranian protesters see Sarsour as more of a threat to their campaign than right-wing conservative Westerners.

Sarsour was met with more backlash following the sentencing of human rights lawyer Nasrin Sotoudeh on March 6, 2019. #BackOffLinda made a comeback after Sarsour tweeted an article from Amnesty International highlighting Sotoudeh's arrest and sentencing:

@lsarsour: Nothing is more dangerous and threatening to powerful men than a bold woman who defends other women. This is a travesty of justice. (2019)

Iranian men and women activists responded to Sarsour's tweet about Sotoudeh by invoking the hashtag #BackOffLinda, including prominent Iranian activist Maryam Shariatmadari:

@Maryamshariatm: Nasrin Sotoudeh was my attorney after I got beaten & arrested b/c of protesting against #ShariaLaw & mandatory hijab. In prison my interrogators were beating me & shouting that even in the West they honor Sharia Law! It's hard to see @lsarsour using her name. #BackOffLinda. (Shariatmadari, 2019)

Later @maryamshariatm, among other Twitter users, labeled Sarsour as a #ShariaLaw supporter.

@Baharak_Irani: As an Iranian/American woman who is very familiar with discriminatory Shariah laws & had experienced violence under Islamic regime in #Iran. I have one msg for false feminists such as @lsarsour @ Ilhan @RashidaTlaib in U.S. "Just Back Off." You're a disgrace to women #BackOffLinda. (Baharak, 2019)

Another former client of Soutdeh's expressed similar sentiments:

> @SalmanSima: Nasrin Sotoudeh advocates human rights. Attorney of women prosecuted in Iran for opposing mandatory hijab. She bravely defended them. She opposes the anti-semite regime that supports evil Hamas. Nasrin was my lawyer too & I won't let terrorists shield under her name #BackOFFLinda. (Sima, 2019)

In the tweets above, Sarsour is characterized as a Sharia law supporter, a "terrorist," and "a disgrace to women" to rebuke Sarsour's misrepresentation of reality—the reality being that while Sarsour appears to show support for Sotoudeh, she simultaneously remains silent on the women of #WhiteWednesdays. Depictions of Sarsour reflected news discourse, creating a binary debate that situated the hijab either as a symbol of oppression or empowerment. Twitter, therefore, at times, reinforced news media narratives rather than presenting alternative discourses.

Another U.S. political actor under the evaluation of Twitter users was U.S. representative Ilhan Omar. The day before Qasem Soleimani's death was announced on January 3, 2020, Alinejad tweeted the following:

> @AlinejadMasih: IMPORTANT: For many Iranian, Qassem Soleimani was a warmonger who caused massive casualties in Syria. He was no hero to average Iranians who chanted against the country's support for Hezbollah and Hamas. (2020)

Following Soleimani's death, Alinejad published an article in *The Washington Post* titled, "Don't believe Iranian propaganda about the mourning for Soleimani" and appeared on the *Fox News* talk show *The Story with Martha MacCallum* to reiterate the same message featured in her tweet. Soleimani's death became a point of political controversy among Americans and Iranians, with many debating President Trump's decision to approve an American drone attack that killed Soleimani. In a *New York Times* news analysis, David E. Sanger (2020) described the attack as "the riskiest move made by the United States in the Middle East since the invasion on Iraq in 2003." Much of the U.S. Democratic party disapproved of Trump's attack on Soleimani, including U.S. representatives Ilhan Omar and Rashida Tlaib. After Alinejad expressed vocal support for Soleimani's death, three days later, Omar retweeted Eli Clifton, a fellow at *The Nation Institute*, accusing Alinejad of receiving money as a U.S. government contractor:

Alinejad responded with a Twitter thread consisting of ten tweets accusing Omar of bullying her and withholding solidarity and support for Iranian women. Subsequently, Alinejad received an outpouring of support while Omar was met with criticism and rebuke:

@MehrnoushAhmadi: She has been one of the main voices of Iranian people in the December uprising and it's aftermath while the western media kept silence about it. The IRI pouring money into propaganda has served them well. Western leftists are such good and naïve targets. (Ahmadi, 2020)

@halimasalat: There is no comparison between these two women. One has principles, integrity & is a passionate advocate for freedom at costs to her safety & family. That's @AlinejadMasih of #MyCameraMyWeapon, #MyStealthyFreedom & #WhiteWednesdays. And the other is @IlhanMN . . . ah well. (Farahdi, 2020)

@maryamnayebyazd: OMG. Masih Alinejad's an independent activist. She is currently being attacked by many pro-regime and anti-human rights forces. Masih in an Iranian hero who spends her days tirelessly interviewing the families who had loved ones murdered by the regime in Iran. How dare you. (Shariatmadari, 2020)

These Iranians on Twitter are hailing Alinejad as a heroine and coming to her defense when she is accused of being a political pundit for the Trump administration while accusing two hijabi women in the United States (Sarsour and Omar) of withholding support for Iranian women. At this point, Omar and Tlaib were both trending in the news cycle after the U.S. Congress altered regulations to accommodate Omar's hijab while in session (Smith, 2020). The discourse illustrates discontent and resentment among some of the Iranian protesters with American hijabi women in positions of power who chose to prioritize the normalization of hijab in the United States over the fight against compulsory hijab in Iran. Transnational feminism requires mutual respect for each feminist's choices according to their own convictions; however, that component does not appear prevalent in the Twitter discourse.

The #WhiteWednesdays Twitter discourse revealed a tension between transnational feminist language and femonationalist rhetoric. The majority of the Twitter discourse reflected an "us vs. them" framework with both parties changing depending on the context of the event, though predominantly the framework was made up of Muslim women in the global South versus Muslim women in the global North. In some ways, the Twitter discourse reflected aspects of transnational feminism. For instance, Twitter served as a platform to debate transnational feminist politics, where feminists could channel a democratic process to openly disagree in a public forum. Also, a transnational feminist paradigm was reflected in the Twitter discourse highlighting voices from the grassroots campaign while challenging the privi-leged voices of American women in power who are frequently broadcasted on mainstream news. Overall, the Twitter discourse provided much more nuance to the conversation on Islam, feminism, and the hijab even while containing conflicting and sometimes homogenizing views of the Muslim woman's experience.

Throughout the Twitter discourse, Alinejad engages the "anti-geopolitical eye" by using Twitter as a bridge to bring the lived experiences of Iranian women directly to the rest of the world. Alinejad tweets videos of women sharing their stories, documenting their abuse, and calling for solidarity. These tweets challenge the geopolitical eye that looks upon issues in other countries with a distant foreign policy gaze by literally bringing Westerners face-to-face with Iranian women. Twitter also allows Iranians to express the nuance and complexity of their struggle that disengages the "objectivity" of the Western gaze. However, as O'Tuathail (1996) notes, "anti-geopolitics is nevertheless reinscribable as a form of geopolitics" (p. 182). In this case, Alinejad's geopolitical vision includes a demand for Western intervention. By disengaging the objectivity of the Western gaze, the emergence of the "us vs. them" framework makes sense, as the clear victim and perpetra-tor are identified. Throughout this process, Alinejad essentially claims that Westerners are either for Iranian women or against Iranian women, based on their ideology regarding hijab and their vocal support. Alinejad does not leave much room for a gray area, which, subsequently, dismisses a transna-tional feminist framework. However, within the Twitter discourse, Iranian women were able to acknowledge the nuances overlooked by Alinejad.

In terms of solidarity, or lack thereof, from Western feminists, activists like Linda Sarsour refrained from participating in the constructed "us vs. them" framework and chose not to vocalize explicit support for Iranian women to avoid any association with Islamophobic stereotypes. However, by prioritiz-ing the normalization of hijab in Western countries, many Western feminists have ignored the oppression Iranian women face due to compulsory hijab, regardless of the evidence displayed through the #WhiteWednesdays cam-paign. In this case, for women like Sarsour, what is happening at home is more important than what is happening abroad—especially if those events conflict with her political ideology. Yet, Sarsour attempts to show solidarity with the imprisoned Sotoudeh, whose voice is not present in the Twitter dis-course. In addition to Sotoudeh, the others imprisoned without the freedom to speak and those without digital access are being spoken for. The problematic aspect lies in the manipulation of the voiceless experience by the voice of representation. In this case, Alinejad's voice on American news media curbed the voiceless experience to serve the agenda she is after—that is, Western support for #WhiteWednesdays (Spivak, 1985; Hawkesworth, 2006).

Chapter 8

Twitter News Sourcing and Transnational Journalism

A pluralistic society requires diverse voices and perspectives, both of which are underserved in mainstream news media content (Gans, 2011; Schudson, 2011). Even within the illusion of objective journalism, it is impossible to claim neutrality when journalists are required to make a number of subjective decisions—including the sources they choose to interview. Pulitzer Prize-winning journalist Wesley Lowery (2020) argues in his *New York Times* article titled, "A Reckoning Over Objectivity, Led by Black Journalists," that the mainstream news media upholds the status quo by continuing to present whiteness as the "neutral objectivity." He writes:

> The mainstream has allowed what it considers to be objective truth to be decided almost exclusively by white reporters and their mostly white bosses [. . .] the views and inclinations of whiteness are accepted as the objective neutral.

Lowery goes on to argue that black and brown journalists should be given the opportunity to uphold journalism that elicits moral clarity rather than objectivity. If journalists had implemented a more critical form of reporting, perhaps Masih Alinejad would have been forced to speak to the criticisms against her on social media from the women she claimed to represent. In fact, if journalists had interviewed someone besides Alinejad, more light could be shed on the Trump administration's cooptation of the White Wednesdays movement. One source is not enough, no matter how esteemed an activist. A single source is not sufficient for cultivating a pluralistic society and a more global point of view. But the audience is no longer limited to what they can consume on mainstream media. The internet has changed the game, and more sources can speak directly to underrepresented issues and provide more nuance to complex matters too often simplified in mainstream news. Working with sources online can help pave the way for a better practice of journalism.

SOURCES, FIXERS, AND JOURNALISTS

Journalists play a small role in a much larger hierarchy of influence that brings the news to its audience. On an individual level, journalists may be ready to implement more diverse sources into their news stories, but they are also subject to institutional routines that dictate the norms and practices of journalism as a whole (Shoemaker and Reese, 2014). Part of these norms include an emphasis on authoritative sources. However, with the changing landscape of news and the rising influence of online user-generated content, journalists must adapt.

Twitter has developed an increasingly larger role within journalism as a way for journalists to both source and report news (Hermida, 2013). In fact, sourcing from Twitter has become a more normalized practice. Unfortunately, journalists tend to continue seeking out and quoting tweets from politicians, celebrities, and government officials rather than incorporating more civilian voices. Gans (2011) argues for a more representative democracy in journalism which includes what he calls "Bottom-up News"—"stories on how ordinary people are affected by the decisions and acts of high government officials and the rest of the political elite who are journalism's major sources." Moreover, Gans (2011) argues that journalists adopt a representational role so that "the facts and conclusions they report represent the people they are covering" (4)—including those outside their home country. That said, journalists are limited in how much empathy they can cultivate in their audience as they work to explain and construe the meaning of events. But "bottom-up news" sources can help interpret and contextualize issues for an audience that is unfamiliar with such matters, sometimes more effectively than a journalist (Hermida et al., 2014). However, the implied hierarchy of credibility that privileges official and government sources often neglects voices directly impacted by the event or issue reported. The hierarchy of credibility must be challenged. By challenging the hierarchy, journalists would inevitably impose on presuppositions of power practiced by mainstream media, and subsequently, journalistic norms like objectivity, balance, and impartiality. The process of challenging this hierarchy will be further explained in the pages that follow.

Some of those sources directly affected by different events and issues can easily be accessed through social media. Sourcing from social media platforms does not have to be a last resort. Instead, journalists should consider implementing discourses from citizens and local journalists via social media when access and geographical restraints prevent direct interviews—especially when covering events in countries where journalism is restricted or controlled by the government. Many Western news bureaus already utilize social media when covering natural disasters, international emergencies, elections, or any other events that move quickly and produce new information faster than a reporter can (Heim, 2021). However, outside of natural disasters and protests, journalists continue to pull tweets from politicians, celebrities, or other high-profile actors (Broersma and Graham, 2013). The amount of space granted to notorious celebrities and politicians not only neglects citizens' voices but also helps maintain power structures in society (Schudson, 2011). Journalists aid in the construction of reality (Tuchman, 1978) by, as Sigal (1973) puts it, not necessarily reporting "what has happened, but what someone says had happened" (69). Therefore, if journalists are truly advocating for democracy, they cannot let elitist sources continue to construct reality for the rest of the world. Instead, journalists must "offer a wide variety of opinions and perspectives to encourage citizens to choose among them in evaluating public policies" (Schudson, 2011, 153). Otherwise, marginalized voices will continue to be sidelined and rendered meaningless. But we cannot limit criticism to just journalists. After all, as previously noted, journalists are simply following the professional routines and news values in which they were trained (Shoemaker and Reese, 2014). However, as Lowery (2020) argued in his *New York Times* article, those norms do not work if the goal is to represent the whole community. The current practice of journalism that sits atop objectivity neglects the diversity of different social, cultural, and economic contexts: that neglect makes it impossible to uphold the values of journalism. For example, accuracy and fairness are core tenets in excellent journalism. But if journalists cannot recognize the intersections between their subjects and themselves, accuracy and fairness are negated. Specifically, without the inclusion of voices from marginalized communities (especially when the story affects them directly), journalism will fall short of excellence and, instead, continue to cultivate a lack of trust from the public (Ford et al., 2020). This can especially be the case when journalists move into a neighborhood, report on events with a skewed perspective of minorities, and leave without exploring everything that the community has to offer. Members of that community grow skeptical of reporters and start avoiding them and ignoring their work entirely (Maynard, 2005). In the opening of Lowery's (2020) article, he tells a story of being dispatched to a mainly black area of Boston following a stabbing. An older black man questioned Lowery's presence in the neighborhood and expressed his complaints regarding mainstream media's poor coverage of black and brown neighborhoods, too often associating those groups with crime and failing to fully explore the areas they cover. Part of this can be explained by one's faultiness and implicit/explicit biases (Ford et al., 2020). Journalists need to expand their worldview.

Additionally, as noted in the first chapter, journalists are vulnerable to the changing landscape of news, such as abandoning foreign bureaus due to budget issues, increasing citizen journalism, and time constraints (Papacharissi and Oliveira, 2012). Part of the downsizing of foreign bureaus reflects the danger of overseas reporting, particularly after the murders of James Foley and Steven Sotloff in Syria in 2014. Time constraints and a lack of resources that expect journalists to do less with more stem from the commodification of news. These changes have affected the quality of journalism and have led to more reliance on citizen journalists for content, not to mention the growing freelance industry (Hellmueller et al., 2017). These dynamic circumstances generate burnout and a lack of resources for journalists to do their best work—especially within transnational news.

But not all is lost. Journalists can collaborate with citizen journalists, very much like they have done with "fixers" in international news. Fixers are "locals" in the area of reporting that assist the reporter in cultural proficiency. Fixers can help with lodging, transportation, translating, and securing interviews—including government officials (Plaut and Klein, 2019, 1696–1697). In many ways, a fixer serves as the "eyes and ears" of the journalist. Journalists are compelled to trust their fixers and allow them to make connections on their behalf. The fixer is, in no uncertain words, a co-producer. A fixer can be a local journalist, a taxi driver, or a friend of a friend. Ultimately, fixers are essential resources for Western journalists, though, unfortunately, they rarely receive any recognition for their work (Murrell, 2014). That said, if Western journalists are accustomed to relying on locals to capture the story, why would a news outlet depend on one journalist—Masih Alinejad—located in the United States, no less, instead of finding someone on the ground to serve as a source? Granted, the geopolitics between the United States and Iran are precarious, which presents issues of access to sources; however, as showcased throughout the Arab Spring and the 2016 bombings in Brussels, journalists can work around their limitations and take to Twitter to crowdsource information and gather user-generated content—particularly photos and videos.

Again, thinking back to countries with restricted press freedom, Western journalists have a responsibility to work with journalists in other countries to continue to preserve an independent press on a global level. For example, while official news outlets may be monitored by government authorities, journalists in Turkey utilize Facebook and YouTube to circumvent censorship and to communicate with mainstream news outlets in other countries. Additionally, "public broadcasters from France, Germany, the United Kingdom, and the United States teamed up to develop a Turkish-language news channel that would air exclusively on YouTube" (Shahbaz, 2019, para. 17) in order to promote multiple perspectives on current affairs in Turkey. These four Western countries' collaboration with Turkish journalists can serve as a blueprint for Western news bureaus to pursue more coalitions with journalists reporting from autocratic countries.

But journalists are not limited to using other journalists as sources. Twitter has served as a consistent platform for protesters to share dissenting opinions, calling out corrupt regimes or even supporting authoritative regimes. Additionally, members of the regimes themselves have adopted Twitter to sabotage protesters. When living under a repressive regime, it takes courage to express dissent online. These regimes have developed strategies to identify those protesters on social media. That said, Iranian women continue to post on social media, consistently showcasing their own bravery by posting criticism of the Rouhani regime and Islamic leaders. By not acknowledging those women's voices, Western journalists are overlooking a crucial part of the story. When conflicting voices are ignored, the privileged remain in power. But journalists can engage with protesters online and utilize social media's ability to open a door for the disruption of the social hierarchy and traditional forms of sourcing often perpetuated by commercial interests (Hermida et al., 2014). Reporters cannot succumb to the neoliberal myth that profitability is the primary goal of journalism. Rather, journalism is "the production of reliable information and analysis needed for the adequate performance of a democratic society" (Van der Haak et al., 2012, 2925).

Sources are crucial to the shape a story takes and navigates an event or issue not only for the reporter but the audience as well. The voices a journalist chooses to include or exclude from the narrative are critical to the meaning attached to the story. Government sources, institutional elites, and officials have dominated the discourse in news sourcing which, inevitably, constructs a social meaning. However, with the rise of crowdsourcing online and implementing more user-generated content, journalists are growing closer to a more representative form of reporting. For instance, during the Arab Spring protests in Tunisia and Egypt, former NPR journalist, Andy Carvin, served as the primary voice on the ground via Twitter. Carvin's reporting strategy included privileging citizen's voices, or alternative voices, rather than "official" sources when covering the protests. Essentially, Carvin became his own gatekeeper and relied on his own skillset to curate sources for his Twitter coverage on the protests. He garnered messages from activists calling for social change and those sharing their own lived experiences during the protests. While Carvin used a wide array of sources from officials, mainstream media journalists, and institutional elites, at least 50 percent of his retweets were sourced by alternative voices. Carvin's coverage was featured in the *New York Times*, *The Guardian*, and *The Washington Post*. Rather than relying on institutional elites or government sources, he effectively collaborated with alternative voices to diversify the discourse in mainstream news coverage. Carvin's approach to gatekeeping is an important avenue to explore considering the increasing threat against the independent press occurring on a global scale.

Carvin adapted his journalistic practices to work within his circumstances, including his ethical framework. One of the larger questions surrounding Twitter sourcing is the issue of verification. In Carvin's case, he used the retweet function as his primary tool. He would retweet links to news articles asking for verification from protesters on the ground. Moreover, if he came across a livestream or video, he would ask his followers for context rather than assume his own interpretation of the images. Carvin also noted that he is wary of any non-journalists who assume "the language of breaking news" and will reach out to the source for more details, photos, or videos; or he may retweet the information and crowdsource his followers for verification. He is also careful not to lose perspective on the fact that his sources are largely part of the opposition (Silverman, 2011). This is important to recognize because his approach highlights his commitment to producing accurate and transparent news without being led by a national agenda.

One of the key findings in the analysis of Carvin's Twitter coverage was his tendency to retweet the same alternative voices. This practice relates to the rapport a journalist builds with her source—the more often you work with someone, the more credibility they gain. Similarly, this association could also mirror a foreign correspondent's relationship with her fixer. The idea of a reporter curating good journalism on her own is a naïve and arrogant notion. Good journalism is a result of collaboration or, what Van der Haak et al. (2012) call "networked journalism." Networked journalism is "a diffused capacity to record information, share it, and distribute it" (2927). Essentially, the professional nature of journalism is maintained in terms of collecting and interpreting information, but "it is driven by a networked practice dependent on sources, commentaries, and feedback," which can largely be found online (2927). Journalists can crowdsource information online while also contributing their skillset in providing context and making sense out of that information for the audience. Some news networks like the *BBC*, *The Guardian*, and *Al Jazeera* already practice crowdsourcing online and integrating user-generated content into their daily broadcasts. By making this practice a norm, journalists are able to provide a more holistic point of view on a situation—especially those that are international. This practice not only serves the group being reported on but also the audience receiving those reports. Credibility in journalism is waning, and classic tenets like objectivity will not save the day. Rather incorporating a meaningful perspective that is transparent will elevate trust in journalists once again. However, this is not to suggest that journalists should take sides on an issue but rather provide a comprehensive report grounded in analysis (Van der Haak et al., 2012). A transnational approach can help journalists move toward a better way of doing journalism.

TRANSNATIONAL JOURNALISM, ETHICS OF CARE, AND GEOPOLITICS

The transnational approach to journalism borrows from the ethics of care by considering *everyone* the story impacts, not simply the domestic audience, politics, or economy.

Within the conversation around global media ethics, journalists from ex-colonial countries express what Rao and Lee (2005) call the "postcolonial suspicion" (p. 106). Postcolonial suspicion is based on the concern that any discussion on global media ethics will prioritize Western interests. For example, within the U.S. context, journalists' freedom to report the truth is protected under the First Amendment; however, this liberty is only applicable to nation states that qualify as democracies (Hossain and Aucoin, 2018). The freedom to report the truth is not always a privilege granted to those countries where democracy is not the bedrock of society. In authoritarian regimes, reporting the truth can often lead to the death of journalists like former *Washington Post* columnist and Saudi citizen Jamal Khashoggi (Rao and Lee, 2005). Given this reality, it is incumbent upon democratic countries to serve the larger global public with their freedom to report the truth. Though since 2019, attacks on the independent press have grown bolder even in some of the world's most respected democracies with rising populist leaders. After all, "freedom of speech does not always extend to freedom after speech." The threat against press freedom in these open societies becomes a threat against an independent press on a global scale.

With the rise of right-wing populist leaders throughout Europe and the United States, national interest has undermined "democratic principles like press freedom, transparency, and open debate" (Repucci, 2019, para 5). Additionally, in the United States, President Trump's contentious relationship with the press has cultivated an increasing public distrust of journalists. Subsequently, the incentives for becoming a pro-government news outlet are all the more appealing, especially considering the ever-present pressures of "government-backed ownership changes, regulatory and financial pressure, and public denunciation of honest journalists" (para 4, example). However, while democratic nations are seeing a decline in press freedom, countries like Ethiopia, Malaysia, Ecuador, and The Gambia have made democratic progress within their own media environments. After facing years of repression, censorship, and persecution, these four countries have shown their potential to rebound and continue the tradition of independent journalism, and they have proven their right to have a seat at the table when discussing media ethics.

The postcolonial suspicion underscores the failure of Western journalists to accurately and ethically report on countries located on the other side of the global hemisphere—especially within the Middle East. For example, in news coverage of the Syrian refugee crisis in 2015, journalists failed to respectfully cover migrants and instead would often "feature propaganda laid out by politicians" (Hossain and Aucoin, 2018, 198). Furthermore, even when journalists attempted to give voice to the voiceless, they often did so at the expense of those subjects' agency. Journalists need to create space for the refugees' perspectives to be published (Chouliaraki and Stolic, 2017).

The concept of allowing stories to be told through their native lens is crucial to ethical reporting and the ethics of care aids in that endeavor. Gilligan (1982), Steiner (2009), and Buzzanell (2011) each built on the concept of feminist media ethics, eventually leading to the development of an ethics of care. Care ethics was originally conceived as the purview of women—a natural characteristic of their biological sex (Gilligan, 1982). However, Steiner (2009) and Buzzanell (2011) both refuted this gender-specific essentialism and argued that an ethics of care was not so much a natural inclination but rather "an acquired and motivated disposition" (Steiner and Okrusch, 2006). The practice of an ethics of care appears contradictory to normative journalistic values like objectivity, but it does contribute to other values like truthfulness and accuracy, as neutrality and impartiality can neglect important facts. This very characterization of care ethics is what makes it so pertinent to the development of transnational media ethics in journalism.

IN SUPPORT OF A TRANSNATIONAL FRAMEWORK

Adopting a transnational framework in journalism allows for transparency and the acknowledgment of issues both within and across cultures. However, media production cannot ignore the needs of the local audience, such as informing the public of the issues and events that affect them directly. Transnational media must develop the ability to code-switch between their audience's spectrum of perspectives, which can be a difficult practice to master (Athique, 2014). Consider the example of the #WhiteWednesdays movement in Iran. Curating news coverage on the women's movement for a U.S. audience requires journalists to acknowledge and communicate the shifting meanings of hijab within different spaces and cultures. While the hijab in Iran can be seen as oppressive by Westerners, journalists cannot ignore the reality that both hijabi and non-hijabi women advocate for a woman's autonomy, including the *right to choose* hijab in Iran. Furthermore, journalists must situate the political debate around hijab within the current lived experiences of hijabi women in the United States and their campaign to normalize hijab. While one woman may find the hijab tyrannical in Iran, a woman in the United States may find it empowering. Wearing the hijab in the United States can be seen as just as brave as a woman in Iran refusing to wear hijab, as Linda Sarsour argued on *CNN* (Scott, 2018). In an authentic practice of the ethics of care, journalists owe it to their audience to explain the transnational shifts in meaning. By instilling a transnational framework in news coverage of feminist movements in the Middle East, the audience can stay informed without creating binaries about gender, race, and religion.

A transnational framework is also the most beneficial for more adequately informing the audience. Contrary to Kant's theory of ethics—which suggests the establishment of a universal code of moral ethics, regardless of context—Vanacker and Breslin (2011) argue that "Moral agents are not only responsible for their own moral choices but also for the moral development of those with whom one enters in a relationship"—including sources (p. 200). Arguably, if the ethics of care are applied outside of personal relationships, journalists' role as moral agents can affect the moral development of their audience and, consequently, the audience's global outlook. This requires the inclusion of vulnerable and marginalized voices.

Research in mass communication has long suggested that media influence public opinion (Gitlin, 1980; Entman, 1993; Powell, 2011; Elsamni, 2016). Because transnationalism promotes the flourishing of all people, journalists must be well educated in their topics to avoid any misrepresentation that could perpetuate harmful stereotypes. However, if journalists continue to turn to politicians and commentators, who often lack extensive experience with issues affecting marginalized communities, the audience has the potential to consume misinformation (Zagor, 2015).

The relationship between media and audience is often dependent on framing. Journalists utilize framing to organize and interpret the world for their audience (Gitlin, 1980). News frames have both a direct and indirect effect on audience attitude toward different social issues, therefore influencing their support or petition against those social issues (Iyengar,1991). Given the complex meanings that can be derived from a news story, it is imperative that journalists recognize the ethical implications of their decisions, especially when choosing sources for the story. Care ethics speaks directly to those implications. The phases of care include attentiveness, responsibility, competence, and responsiveness (Fisher and Tronto, 1991; Tronto, 1995). Those four components of care should be reflected in journalistic values. The first phase, attentiveness, requires sufficient time invested in gaining knowledge on the story's different elements. By taking this care, journalists must also take into account the consequences of their reporting, particularly those unwillingly involved in the story. Second, journalists do not only have a responsibility to anticipate the potential outcomes of their story, but they are also responsible for those consequences. Journalists must pursue their stories responsibly and utilize their resources both ethically and effectively. Journalists must recognize their position of power and the power of their words. Third, competence and skill are imperative to protecting the subjects involved as well as the craft of journalism. Transnational journalism enables competent, comprehensive, and quality content. Finally, responsiveness. Journalists must respond to circumstances that demand care and respond in instances when they are careless. Within self-absorbed Western individualism and American exceptionalism, it can be difficult for journalists to transition to a transnational journalism paradigm. But the change is imperative.

In the midst of revolutions and feminist movements taking hold in the Middle East, practicing transnationalism in journalism is important for ensuring the production of a holistic narrative that includes the most vulnerable and marginalized voices. Ultra-nationalism cannot guide or inform transnational reporting. This is not to suggest that journalists should not take pride in their country or become stateless, but rather to discourage the tendency to put the country over humanity. A transnational framework does not entertain ethnocentrism but rather embraces the nuances within different cultures, and the way meanings shift within and between those cultures. If the values of journalists are rooted in giving an informed report, to preserve the quality and purpose of journalism, the paradigm needs to change.

Conclusion

The media discourse surrounding #WhiteWednesdays perpetuated a binary narrative of hijab that pits feminists against each other by creating teams of pro/anti-hijab. Though the women involved acknowledge contextual circumstances regarding hijab, to some extent, those same women lean toward the narrative that corroborates their own lived experience—particularly native informants like Ayaan Hirsi Ali, Azar Nafisi, and Mona Eltatawy. Consider the *CNN* interview with Linda Sarsour and Masih Alinejad, where both women held tightly to their respective convictions—Sarsour advocating for Muslim women facing Islamophobia in the United States and Alinejad campaigning for Iranian women protesting against compulsory hijab law. Both women consent to a hierarchy of oppression in which each feminist operates on the notion that their fight is the most important. Hierarchy is not compatible with the transnational feminist paradigm. While both women at some point acknowledge the merit behind each other's campaigns, they are also working to tip the mediated narrative in their favor. Thus, the mediated discourse on hijab is shaped within an "us vs. them" framework that negates transnational feminism and instead creates a platform for both orientalist and femonationalist rhetoric to emerge.

The general issue with the platform of mainstream news media outlets is the limited framework through which complex issues can be fleshed out. The way the binary narrative on hijab is presented to the audience is an oversimplified description of the larger controversy. Though, the oversimplification could be a strategy to distract the audience from the political context of the resistance movement. There is little room or time to sufficiently expand on the political, cultural, and geographical nuances that bring us to the moment of debate, let alone give the audience reason to invest in the issue at all—which is why framing is so important. All six of the news outlets included in the case study represent one thing—hegemonic power. News media have the power to choose who tells stories and how they get told—often highlighting elite sources that value authority over authenticity—featuring limited visions of the truth that excludes information that does not fit the political agenda (Farris, 2017). Throughout the news coverage of #WhiteWednesdays, reporters relied on privileged voices of well-known, predominantly Western-based activists with problematic reputations as well as elitist men from Muslim organizations who do not have the authority or lived experience to speak to different framings of hijab. However, these are the sources that reign over the hierarchy of credibility and, ultimately, define not only the issue but also the interpretation of that issue communicated through the journalists that interview them (Hermida et al., 2014). By defaulting to elite sources and sidestepping voices from the ground, the message claiming to support those under-privileged voices is hollow. The very exclusion of less privileged voices renders them invisible and maintains the hegemonic geopolitical eye that creates distance between the elite and the ordinary (Pande and Nadkami, 2016). After all, how can the audience be expected to understand the context of issues outside the Western world when the news is consistently relayed through a Western lens?

While producers relied heavily on Alinejad to represent the Iranian woman's perspective, the oversimplified narrative of the Muslim woman progresses. In the beginning, Alinejad did qualify as a part of the proletariat representing the grassroots protest on the ground. She made some brave choices to carve out a career in journalism while living in Iran before she was exiled. She initiated the My Stealthy Freedom movement and, following Movahed's protest in Tehran, created the #WhiteWednesdays campaign. For news producers and journalists, Alinejad serves as the ideal representative of Iranian women. Ultimately, she is working to eradicate compulsory hijab and, by default, a woman's right to choose. However, as Alinejad's cultural capital continued to grow as a digital activist, inevitably, so did her privilege, granting her access to avenues of power previously out of reach.

As the U.S. government worked with Alinejad to discuss possible options for supporting the women in Iran, Alinejad's mediated discourse was adjusted to tell a specific story about hijab that only promoted certain rights for some women in exchange for political support (Fenton, 2015). Alinejad shifted her argument away from a narrative focused on women's choice to publicizing a vendetta against the hijab, primarily featured on right-wing news media outlet *Fox News*. The news discourse, especially from *Fox News* and *USA Today*, aligned with the United States' geopolitical agenda to use women's rights as a portal to intervene in Iranian affairs as it once did during the 1953 coup organized by the CIA. The relationship between social movement leaders and government entities is a precarious one that has the potential to cultivate ethical issues. While it is necessary for protesters to work with imperialist government entities to ensure systemic changes, it is when protesters work for and are paid by those "imperialist" government entities that things become complicated—like Alinejad's role as a journalist for Voice of America (a U.S. government–funded entity). The capitalist dimension of this relationship must be eliminated for Alinejad to maintain authenticity as a representative for the #WhiteWednesdays campaign.

The largest difference between the news and Twitter discourse was the diversity of sources included in the conversation on #WhiteWednesdays. From the beginning of #WhiteWednesdays, Alinejad showcased her ability to reconfigure Twitter to challenge the geopolitical eye by transferring up-close and personal images of women in Iran being harassed, arrested, and beaten for not wearing proper hijab to the global public sphere. Alinejad and the women of #WhiteWednesdays made the anti-geopolitical eye possible by carving out their own space on Twitter for their voices to be heard. Additionally, Iranian and Iranian American feminists utilized Twitter to support and challenge the mediated discourses circulated by Alinejad and others like Sarsour and Omar—all high-profile, privileged women advocating for Muslim women in different ways. In this way, Twitter served as a space for transnational feminism to inhabit—a space where debates on feminism circulated, deterring the homogenization of any one woman or struggle. However, only some of these discourses make it to the mainstream news conversation. Furthermore, #WhiteWednesdays also featured feminist critiques of Western feminist expressions of solidarity with Muslim women. Within this space, Iranian women who do and do not wear hijab challenged those manifestations of solidarity that reflected orientalist tropes exaggerating the role of hijab. Within the Twitter discourse, Iranian women brought political, cultural, and geographical context and nuance to the practice of hijab and to feminism as a whole.

However, platforms for alternative-activist new media do not always challenge hegemonic ideologies and institutions. In the case of #WhiteWednesdays, the Twitter discourse often reinforced hegemonic structures. The reflection of hegemonic narratives within the Twitter discourse resurrected the issue of power in social movements. While a social movement can use social media to gain momentum, popularity, and global reach, without access to institutions with political power, little can be done to influence radical change. Alinejad successfully placed the campaign in conversation with institutions of power—in this case, American news media. While Iranian Twitter used the platform to interact with news media from all over the world, there is little evidence that U.S. mainstream news media responded—with the exception of *The Washington Post* via Alinejad and Iranian American reporter Roya Hakakian. For the most part, Iranians only responded to articles written or promoted by Alinejad—again, an example of their commitment to hold Alinejad accountable as a representative of Iranian women. Those articles written by Alinejad and Hakakian also exemplify the shift from a campaign once built on the voices of the Iranian people to the hands of white, Western conglomerates who can utilize the movement to maintain their infrastructures of power. Once the objective changes, so does the voice.

Both the news discourse and the Twitter discourse revealed an overall binary narrative; however, the Twitter platform allowed for more debate and acknowledgment of nuance, context, and debate in a way that was not possible—or at least not present—on a news platform. Yet, the hyper-focused discourse on hijab in *Fox News* also emerged within Twitter narratives about Linda Sarsour, the Women's March, and expressions of solidarity. Additionally, voices from Iranian feminists who were arrested, subjected to violence, and expressed a distrust of Islam mirrored the femonationalist language from segments like *The Five*, *Tucker Carlson Tonight*, and *The Story with Martha MacCallum*. Moreover, those Iranian feminists showed little concern for the appropriation of the #WhiteWednesdays campaign by alt-right political commentators. Instead, more attention was directed at "fake feminists" (i.e., Linda Sarsour, Ilhan Omar) who withheld support from #WhiteWednesdays and were believed to misrepresent Muslim women in an attempt to further their own political agendas in the United States. In some cases, the femonationalist rhetoric projected on conservative news outlets aligned with the ideology of some of the protesters.

The #WhiteWednesdays case study confirms that the supposed credibility of the message may be dependent on the medium—at least as long as journalists continue to overlook grassroots voices in favor of elite sources, which are inevitably an extension of the social institutions that grassroots movements aim to change. It is imperative to grant more attention to alternative platforms where more voices can be heard if news producers and journalists are truly dedicated to serving as the fourth estate that accurately, effectively, and ethically works for the benefit of the public. Since Twitter has risen in popularity as a source for both journalists and audiences alike, news reporting is gradually incorporating Twitter discourse for a more authentic view of social movements—as seen throughout coverage of the Arab Spring (Hermida, Lewis, and Smith, 2014). More research on the credibility, authenticity, and utility of the incorporation of Twitter discourse from protesters is needed. The context available through these sources is invaluable to challenging the geopolitical eye—bringing the "far away" closer.

Previous literature on orientalism and more recent scholarship of neo-orientalism (Said, 1978, 1980; Mishra, 2007; Seddighi and Tafakori, 2016; Chugarti, 2017; Hasan, 2018) explores the lack of context in U.S. news when reporting on women's issues in Islamic countries, but little research exists on the geopolitical consequences for the way those issues are reported in mainstream news. The existing scholarship focuses on Muslim women finding themselves reported on consistently through a patriarchal lens—white men liberating brown women from brown men only to be shifted from one patriarchal context to the next. Furthermore, the literature delves into how the patriarchy weaponizes and manipulates women's movements in the global South for its own satisfaction—maintaining neoliberal infrastructures of power, media imperialism, the modernization agenda, and so on. But not enough of this conversation is taking place in the realm of communication and journalism studies. Instead, the emphasis continues to be put on the technological aspect of the argument—Does social media give voice to the colonized? Can social media evolve into a liberated infrastructure? Does social media influence radical change? Social media is the medium. But, as exemplified in this case study, the medium is hardly the issue. The problem does not lie within the power social media does or does not hold. The problem is who is wielding the power. As long as the privileged maintain power, marginalized voices will be null and void.

Research on femonationalism is slowly emerging within feminist studies but is absent from scholarship on communication and journalism—where femonationalist rhetoric often resides. As countries continue to use populism to promote dangerous forms of nationalism, femonationalism is a credible threat emerging within the United States as well as other Western countries. Real-world consequences exist. The #WhiteWednesdays case study looks to the geopolitical consequences likely to transpire between the United States and Iran, most recently the killing of Iranian general Qasem Soleimani in January 2020. Following Soleimani's death, American actress and Me Too activist Rose McGowan tweeted the following:

> Dear #Iran, The USA has disrespected your country, your flag, your people. 52% of us humbly apologize. We want peace with your nation. We are being held hostage by a terrorist regime. We do not know how to escape. Please do not kill us. #Soleimani (2020)

The tweet has since been deleted after McGowan received numerous attacks on Twitter directing her to Alinejad's profile as well as #WhiteWednesdays. Twitter users used McGowan's tweet as an opportunity to make the point that the #MeToo movement does not care for any women outside the Western context—hence McGowan's ignorance of the campaign. The #WhiteWednesdays movement is then used as justification for Soleimani's death.

The Trump administration accused American feminists of withholding support from Iranian women because of their loyalties to former president Barack Obama and his participation in the Nuclear Deal. The discourse that once highlighted women's rights issues in Iran eventually overshadowed the movement with the voices of privileged sources who did little to speak for the women seeking freedom. With Alinejad's help, ironically, the anti-geopolitical eye cultivated by the women of #WhiteWednesdays became submerged under U.S. foreign policy—enabling U.S. economic sanctions against Iran, damaging Iranian women's financial and social independence as entrepreneurs (Moaveni and Vaez, 2020). Furthermore, the Trump administration's continued politicization of women's rights in Iran ignores discrimination against women in other Muslim countries such as Saudi Arabia, a close political ally of the United States. Perhaps the Trump administration used the #WhiteWednesdays movement as a strategy to encourage regime change in Iran.

In terms of transnational feminist scholarship, more studies on expressions of solidarity must be carried out, as well as work focused on dispelling the binary narrative on hijab—which sustains the Western obsession with the veil. If Muslim women are debating the symbol of hijab, Westerners will, subsequently, maintain the problematic image of a single-dimension Muslim woman clad in an American flag hijab. Likewise, as Azadi (2015) notes, the solidarity offered by Western feminists who wear hijab, while well-intentioned, produces more harm than good because it also continues to sustain the association of Muslim women with hijab, again ignoring the diversity of Muslim women around the world. Instead, Azadi (2015) suggests that the best performance of solidarity is to provide space for marginalized communities to speak on behalf of themselves.

While journalists can do their best to communicate events and help their audience understand those events, without the lived experiences of women on the ground, their empathy is limited. Consequently, those audiences consuming the journalist's rendition of the events internalize a narrower vision of a much larger context. The audience may be moved and inspired by the stories broadcasted and published in the news media, but their engagement with the group affected is implemented on their own terms and their own understanding of the events. In today's era of social media activism, many audiences in the global North are galvanized by social movements in the global South—campaigns that most Westerners have little to no experience with. Because of their well-intentioned ignorance, the way some Westerners show solidarity with women in the global South is often flawed. For example, the women in New Zealand's choice to wear headscarves in solidarity with victims from the Christ Church shooting unintentionally excluded those Muslim women who do not wear hijab. Likewise, Western nationalists who consume limited information on the #WhiteWednesdays campaign from the news source of their choice can misunderstand those events as a crusade against Islam and perpetuate femonationalist rhetoric with the intention of showing support for

Iranian women. The voice of one woman with access to white, Western men with power is not enough to accomplish radical change but rather further strengthens infrastructures of power. Power must be redistributed before radical change can occur (Fenton, 2015). Radical change starts to come into view when the voices of the less powerful, the less privileged, and the ones with the least amount of access are amplified.

The amplification of marginalized voices is a critical step for journalists covering complex issues like Muslim women's experience with hijab. Not only must journalists diversify their sources, they must make the extra effort to seek out sources in nonconventional ways. Journalists' use of Twitter is becoming a more normalized practice in reporting, especially since the events surrounding the Arab Spring in 2011 (Hermida et al., 2014). But in this case, there was no evidence of American journalists seeking out Iranian women's voices outside of Alinejad's—whose narrative can be illustrated as an inspiring one but only tells one side of the story. In the same way that American feminists must recognize the multidimensional Muslim woman, journalists must acquire the voices of all of those women to fight against stereotypical archetypes. American feminists and journalists are not called to appropriate cultural and/or religious symbols to support Muslim women, but they are required to make sure that the diverse voices of those women are heard. The research on femonationalism and #WhiteWednesdays is far from over as we await the release of the imprisoned women in Iran, the future of the contentious relationship between the United States and Iran, as well as the inevitably shifting discourse on the campaign moving forward. As femonationalist rhetoric continues to grow alongside hate crimes against Muslims and other minorities in the Western world, the time for a paradigm shift is now.

Bibliography

Abdelaziz, Salma. 2019. *CNN Newsroom*. Atlanta, GA: CNN.

Abrahamian, Atossa. 2017. "Who's Afraid of Linda Sarsour?" *The Fader.com*, April 17, 2017. https://www.thefader.com/2017/04/27/linda-sarsour-interview-feminism -sharia-womens-march

Abu-Lughod, Lila. 2013. *Do Muslim Women Need Saving?* Cambridge: Harvard University Press.

Abu-Lughod, Lila and Rabab El-Mahdi. 2011. "Beyond the "Woman Questions" in the Egyptian Revolution." *Feminist Studies*, *37*(3), 683–691. https://www.jstor.org /stable/23069928

AHA Foundation, The. 2021. "About Us." https://www.theahafoundation.org/about-us/

Al-Ali, Nadje and Nicole Pratt. 2009. *What Kind of Liberation? Women and the Occupation of Iraq*. Berkeley, CA: University of California Press.

Albrow, Martin. 1990. "Introduction." In *Globalization, Knowledge and Society*, edited by Martin Albrow and Elizabeth King, 3–16. London: Sage.

Al Maghlooth, A. A. 2014. *The Relevance of Gatekeeping in the Process of Contemporary News Creation and Circulation in Saudi Arabia*. PhD thesis, Media & Cultural Studies. Greater Manchester: University of Salford.

Alinejad, Masih. 2018. *The Wind in My Hair*. New York: Little, Brown and Company.

Alinejad, Masih. 2019 October 7. "My Brother Ali is Iran's Latest Hostage." *WallStreetJournal.com*. https://www.wsj.com/articles/my-brother-ali-is-irans-la test-hostage-11570389518

Alinejad, Masih. 2020 January 6. "Don't Believe Iranian Propaganda about the Mourning for Soleimani." *WashingtonPost.com*. https://www.washingtonpost.com /opinions/2020/01/06/dont-believe-iranian-propaganda-about-mourning-soleimani/

Alinejad, Masih. [@AlinejadMasih]. 2018, July 5. *I'm Giving an Interview to an #Italianmagazine about Federica Mogherini Who Betrayed #Iranian People, Especially #Women, for the Sake*. [Tweet]. Twitter.twitter.com/alinejadmasih/s tatus/1014882573816942594?lang=en.

Alinejad, Masih. [@AlinejadMasih]. 2019. *I Call on Belgian and Other Western News Outlets As Well As All Feminists in the World to Condemn The.* Twitter, March 12, 2019. https://twitter.com/alinejadmasih/status/1127698200633257984

Alinejad, Masih. [AlinejadMasih]. 2019. *Now I Call on New Zealand Women to Show Their Sisterhood and Solidarity With Us, Who Are Being Beaten Up.* Twitter, March 26, 2019. twitter.com/AlinejadMasih/status/1110654398508 748804t

Alinejad, Masih. [@AlinejadMasih]. 2019. *When I Appeared in Vogue Some Leftists Attacked & Said Anti Compulsory Hijab Campaigner Can't be in a Capitalist Fashion.* Twitter, March 30, 2019. twitter.com/alinejadmasih/status/1112077 319651368963?lang=en

Alinejad, Masih. [@AlinejadMasih]. 2020, January 2. *IMPORTANT: For Many Iranian, Qassem Soleimani was a Warmonger Who Caused Massive Casualties in Syria. He was No Hero To.* Twitter, January 2, 2020. https://twitter.com/Aline jadMasih/status/1212915124664782848

Alinejad, Masih and Roya Hakakian. 2019 April 7. "There Are Two Types of Hijabs: The Difference is Huge." *Washington Post.* https://www.washingtonpost.com/opin ions/global-opinions/there-are-two-types-of-hijabs-the-difference-is-huge/2019/04 /07/50a44574-57f0-11e9-814f-e2f46684196e_story.html

Al-Rasheed, Madawi. 2013. *A Most Masculine State: Gender, Politics and Religion in Saudi Arabia.* Cambridge University Press.

Al-Sharif, Manal. 2017. "I Can't Wait to Drive in Saudi Arabia Again." *New York Times,* September 27, 2018. https://nyti.ms/2yu9tW3

Amir-Khan, Tariq. 2012. "New Orientalism, Securitization and the Western Media's Incendiary Racism." *Third World Quarterly, 33*(9), 1595–1610. DOI: 10.1080/01436597.2012.720831

Amir Mohamad. [@AmirMohamad474]. 2019. *Iranian Women Have Been Oppressed for So Long, and They Deserve a Voice, However It's Unfortunate that You Have Been.* Twitter, February 4, 2019. Account suspended.

Aouragh, Miriyam. 2012. "Social Media, Mediation and the Arab Revolutions." *Triple C, 10*(2), 518–536.

Arnsperger, Christian and Yanis Varoufakis. 2003. "Toward a Theory of Solidarity." *Erkenntnis, 59,* 157–188. DOI: 10.1023/A:1024630228818

Askar, Moradi. [@MoradiAskar]. 2019. *The Duplicity of Western Politicians Is Well Known, It Has Nothing To Do with Human Rights and Freedom. To Do.* Twitter, March 27, 2019. twitter.com/MoradiAskar/status/1110832128860848129

Atad, Erga. 2017. "Global Newsworthiness and Reversed Domestication." *Journalism Practice, 11*(6), 760–776. DOI: 10.1080/17512786.2016.1194223

Athique, Adrian. 2013. "Transnational Audiences: Geocultural Approaches." *Continuum, 1,* 4–17. DOI: 10.1080/10304312.2014.870868

Atosa. [@atosa24]. 2018. *@lsarsour Shut up Linda! We Iranian Women Know Too Well What "Real Islam" Is! We Also Know Too Well Who.* Twitter, January 18, 2018. https://twitter.com/atosa24/status/954130065008332801

Atton, Chris. 2002. *Alternative Media.* Thousand Oaks, CA: Sage Publications.

Azadi, Farah. 2015. "Solidarity and 'The Veil': Why Wearing a Hijab in Solidarity is More Complicated Than You Think." *Stealthishijab.com.* https://stealthishijab.co

m/2015/12/14/solidarity-and-the-veil-why-wearing-a-hijab-in-solidarity-is-more-c omplicated-than-you-think/

Bagnied, Magda and Steven Schneider. 1981. "Sadat Goes to Jerusalem: Televised Images, Themes, and Agenda." In *Television Coverage of the Middle East*, edited by William C. Adams, 53–75. New Jersey: Ablex Publishing Corporation.

Baharak. [@Baharak_Irani]. 2019. *As an Iranian/American Woman Who is Very Familiar with Discriminatory Shariah Laws & Had Experienced Violence under Islamic Regime.* Twitter, March 13, 2019. https://twitter.com/Baharak_Irani/status /1105962195366621186

Bahramitash, Roksana. 2005. *Liberation from Liberalization: A Gender Perspective on Southeast Asia.* London: Zed Books.

Bahri, Mitra. [@mitrabahri]. 2019, February 4. *@Alinejadmasih and @SecPompeo How Could You Dare Even Imagining That You are the Voice of Iranian People When They Are.* Twitter, February 4, 2019. twitter.com/mitrabahri/status/1092578841959243777

Barkho, Leon. 2011. "The Role of Internal Guidelines in Shaping News Narratives: Ethnographic Insights into the Discursive Rhetoric of Middle East Reporting by the BBC and Al-Jazeera English." *Critical Discourse Studies*, 8(4), 297–309. DOI: 10.1080/17405904.2011.601642

Barnett, Clive and David Land. 2007. "Geographies of Generosity: Beyond the 'Moral Turn'." *Geoforum*, *38*, 1065–1075.

Barron, Laignee. 2018. "'A Revolutionary Moment': Activist Mona Eltahawy Talks Sexual Assault, Self-defense and #MosqueMeToo." *Time*, March 7, 2018. https:// time.com/5170236/mona-eltahawy-mosquemetoo/

Basu, Amrita. 1995. *The Challenge of Local Feminisms. Women's Movements in Global Perspective.* San Francisco, CA: Westview Press.

Bayat, Asef. 2010. *Life as Politics: How Ordinary People Change the Middle East.* Stanford: Stanford University Press.

BBC News. 2018. "Iran Protests: Why is There Unrest?" *BBC*, January 2, 2018. https ://www.bbc.com/news/world-middle-east-42544618

Beck, Ulrich. 2006. *Cosmopolitan Vision.* Cambridge: Polity.

Berglez, Peter. 2007. "For a Transnational Mode of Journalistic Writing." In *Ideological Horizons in Media and Citizen Discourses: Theoretical and Methodological Approaches*, edited by Birgitta Höijer, 147–161. Göteborg: Nordicom.

Berglez, Peter. 2008. "What is Global Journalism? Theoretical and Empirical Conceptualization." *Journalism Studies*, 9(6), 845–858. DOI: 10.1080/146167 00802337727

Berglez, Peter. 2013. *Global Journalism: Theory and Practice.* New York: Peter Lang Inc.

Boniadi, Nazanin. 2018. "Actress: Iranian Women are Breaking Their Silence—and Deserve Our Support." *CNN*, February 6, 2018. https://www.cnn.com/2018/02/06/ opinions/iran-global- women-rights-opinion-boniadi/index.html

Brenner, Johanna. 2003. "Transnational Feminism and the Struggle for Global Justice." *New Politics*, 9(2), 78–87. DOI: 10.2307/20459120

Broersma, Marcel and Todd Graham. 2013. "Twitter as A News Source: How Dutch and British Newspapers Used Tweets In their News Coverage, 2007–2011."*Journalism Practice*, *4*, 446–464. DOI: 10.1080/17512786.2013.802481

Buchanan, Rose Troup. 2018. "The Image of a Woman without Her Headscarf in Iran Isn't from the Current Protests Here's Why." *Buzzfeed*, January 3, 2018. https://ww w.buzzfeednews.com/article/rosebuchanan/iran-hijab-old-picture

Bulman, M. 2018. "Iranian Woman Who Removed Headscarf Jailed for Two Years." *The Independent*, March 9, 2018. https://www.independent.co.uk/news/world /middleeast/iran-woman-headscarf-take-off-hijab-remove-jailed-prison-tehran -enghelab-a8246076.html

Butler, Judith. 2018. *Notes toward a Performative Theory of Assembly*. Cambridge, MA: Harvard University Press.

Buzzanell, Patrice. 2011. "Feminist Discursive Ethics." In *The Handbook of Communication Ethics*, edited by George Cheney, Steve May, and Debashish Munshi, 64–83, New York, NY: Routledge.

Care for Brain. [@careforbrain]. 2019. *@AlinejadMasih and @SecPompeo What a Great News. Iran Needs a Regime Change and We Need More Support from the Rest*. Twitter, February 4, 2019 twitter.com/care4brain/status/109252859011207 9875

Caron, Christina and Maya Salam. 2018. "Macy's Courts Muslims with New Hijab Brand." *New York Times*, February 8, 2018. https://www.nytimes.com/2018/02/08/ business/macys-hijabs.html

Carvalho, Anabella. 2008. "Media(ted) Discourse and Society: Rethinking the Framework of Critical Discourse Analysis." *Journalism Studies*, 9(2), 162–177. DOI: 10.1080/14616700701848162

Castells, Manuel. 2015. *Networks of Outrage and Hope: Social Movements in the Internet Age*. Malden, MA: Polity Press.

Change for Equality. 2006. "Petition: International Support for Women's Campaign." http://www.campaignforequality.info/english/spip.php?article19

Chouliaraki, Lilie and Tijana Stolic. 2017. "Rethinking Media Responsibility in the Refugee 'Crisis': A Visual Typology of European News." *Media, Culture & Society*, 39(8), 1162–1177. DOI: 10.1177/0163443717726163

Christians, Clifford G. and John C. Merrill. 2009. *Ethical Communication: Moral Stances in Human Dialogue*. Columbia: University of Missouri.

Chughtai, Alia. 2017. "US-Saudi Relations: A Timeline." *Al Jazeera*, May 18, 2017. https://www.aljazeera.com/indepth/interactive/2017/05/saudi-relations-timeline-1 70518112421011.html

Comor, Edward and James Compton. 2015. "Journalistic Labour and Technological Fetishism." *The Political Economy of Communication*, 3(2) 74–87.

Council on Foreign Relations. 2018. "U.S.-Saudi Relations." *Council on Foreign Relations*. December 7, 2018. https://www.cfr.org/backgrounder/us-saudi-arabia -relations

Crenshaw, Kimberle. 1991. "Mapping the Margins: Intersectionality, Identity Politics, and Violence against Women of Color." *Stanford Law Review*, 43(6), 1241–1299. https://doi.org/10.2307/1229039

Cummings, Judith. 1979. "Demonstrates in City Back Iranian Women's Rights." *New York Times*. March 16, 1979. https://nyti.ms/1OXbXSl

Dabashi, Hamid. 2011. *Brown Skin White Masks*. Chicago: Pluto Press.

Dale, Helle. 2012. "Why America Has Trouble Reaching Iran: VOA's Persian News Network in Dire Need of Reform." *The Heritage Foundation*, March 5, 2012. https ://www.heritage.org/global-politics/report/why-america-has-trouble-reaching-iran voas-persian-news-network-dire-need

Dardot, Pierre and Christian Laval. 2013. *The New Way of the World: On Neo-Liberal Society*. New York: Verso.

Davidson, Joyce, Liz Bondi and Mick Smith. 2016. *Emotional Geographies*. England, UK: Routledge.

Davis, Aaron C. 2010. "Contractor Whose Death Trump Cited was a Naturalized U.S. Citizen Born in Iraq." *Washington Post*. January 7, 2010. https://www.washingt onpost.com/investigations/contractor-whose-death-trump-cites-was-a-naturalized-us -citizen-born-in-iraq/2020/01/07/afa7e774-31ac-11ea-91fd-82d4e04a3fac_story.html

Deeb, Lara. 2006. *An Enchanted Modern: Gender and Public Piety in Shi'i Lebanon*. Princeton University Press.

Dehghan, Saeed Kamali. 2018. "Second Woman Arrested in Tehran for Hijab Protest." *The Guardian*, January 29, 2018. https://www.theguardian.com/world/2 018/jan/29/second-woman-arrested-tehran-hijab-protest-iran

Della Porta, Donatella. 2006. *Globalization From Below: Transnational Activists and Protest Networks*. Minneapolis, MN: University of Minnesota Press.

Della Porta, Donatella, and Sidney Tarrow. 2004. *Transnational Protest and Global Activism*. Lanham, MD: Rowman & Littlefield.

Dencik, Lina. 2013. "What Global Citizens and Whose Global Moral Order? Defining the Globalat BBC World News." *Global Media and Communication*, *9*(2), 119–134. DOI: 10.1177/1742766513479716

den Drömmare, D. [@Dora_kula]. *I'm an Iranian Feminist and I Don't Support @ lsarsour Who Says Hijab Empowers Women. This is Dangerously Distorted from the*. [Tweet]. Twitter.

Deuze, Mark. 2006. "Participation, Remediation, Bricolage: Considering Principal Components of a Digital Culture." *The Information Society*, *22*(2), 63–75. DOI: 10.1080/01972240600567170

Douai, Aziz. 2013. "'Seeds of Change' in Tahrir Square and Beyond: People Power or Technological Convergence?" *American Communication Journal*, *15*(1), 24–33.

Downing, John D. H. 2001. *Radical Media: Rebellious Communication and Social Movements*. Thousand Oaks, CA: Sage Publications.

Durham, Meenakshi Gigi. 2014. "Scene of the Crime: News Discourse of Rape in India and the Geopolitics of Sexual Assault." *Feminist Media Studies*, *15*(2), 175–191. DOI: 10.1080/14680777.2014.930061

Elsamni, Abdulrahman. 2016. "Threat of the Downtrodden: The Framing of Arab Refugees on CNN." *Arab Media & Society*, *22*, 1–18.

Elsen-Ziya, Hande. 2013. "Social Media and Turkish Feminism: New Resources for Social Activism." *Feminist Media Studies*, *13*(5), 860–870. DOI: 10.1080/14680777.2013.838369

Eltahawy, Mona. 2012. "Why Do They Hate Us? The Real War on Women is in The Middle East." *Foreign Policy*, April 23, 2012. https://foreignpolicy.com/2012/04 /23/why-do-they-hateus/

Eltahawy, Mona. 2015. *Headscarves and Hymens: Why the Middle East Needs a Sexual Revolution.* New York: Harper Collins Publishers.

Eltantawy, Nahed. 2013. "From Veiling to Blogging: Women and Media in the Middle East." *Feminist Media Studies, 13*(5), 765–769. DOI: 10.1080/14680777.2013.838356

Entman, Robert M. 1993. "Framing: Toward Clarification of a Fractured Paradigm." *Journal ofCommunication, 43*(4), 51–58.

Entman, Robert M. 2003. *Projections of Power: Framing News, Public Opinion, and U.S. Foreign Policy.* Chicago: University of Chicago Press.

Etehad, Melissa and Nabih Bulos. 2017. "Allowing Women to Drive is Expected to Boost Saudi Arabia's Economy." *LA Times.* October 1, 2017. http://www.latimes.com/world/middleeast/la-fg-saudi-arabia-driving-2017-story.html

Fairclough, Norman. 2003. *Analysing Discourse: Textual Analysis for Social Research.* London: Routledge.

Falcón, Sylvanna. M. 2016. "Transnational Feminism as a Paradigm for Decolonizing the Practice of Research." *Frontiers: A Journal of Women Studies, 37*(1), 174–194. https://www.jstor.org/stable/10.5250/fronjwomestud.37.1.0174#metadata_info_tab_contents

Fang, Lee. 2020. "VOA Persian Awarded Journalism Contract to Controversial Former Trump Campaign Operative." *The Intercept,* January 7, 2020. https://theintercept.com/2020/01/07/voa-persian-iran-trump-conflict-of-interest/

Farahdi, Sharshalimar. [@sharshalimar]. 2019. *Visit Iran as True Sisters and Start a Real Protest by Taking Off Your Head Scarf Then You Show Solidarity With Muslim Women.* Twitter, March 27, 2019.twitter.com/sharshalimar/status/1110809073270833157

Farris, Sara R. 2017. *In the Name of Women's Rights: The Rise of Femonationalism.* Durham: Duke University Press Books.

Featherstone, David. 2012. *Solidarity: Hidden Histories and Geographies of Internationalism.* London: Zed Books.

Fenton, Natalie. 2015. "Left Out? Digital Media, Radical Politics and Social Change." *Information Communication and Society, 19*(3), 346–361. DOI: 10.1080/1369118X.2015.1109698

Fenton, Natalie. 2016. *Digital. Political. Radical.* John Wiley & Sons.

Fernandes, Leela. 2013. *Transnational Feminism in the United States: Knowledge, Ethics, Power.* New York, NY: New York University Press.

Ferree, Myra Marx and Aili M. Tripp. 2006. *Global Feminism: Transnational Women's Activism, Organizing, and Human Rights.* New York, NY: New York University Press.

Finkel, Jori. 2018. "Mediating Faith and Style: Museums Awake to Muslim Fashions." *New York Times,* September 25, 2018. https://www.nytimes.com/2018/09/25/arts/design/de-young-museum-contemporary-muslim-fashions.html

Fisher, Berenice and Joan Tronto. 1990. "Toward a Feminist Theory of Caring." In *Circles of Care: Work and Identity in Women's Lives,* edited by Emily K. Abel and Margaret K. Nelson, 35–62. Albany: SUNY Press.

Flynn, Donna K. 1997. "Trading Traitors: Cultural Negotiations of Female Mobility in a West African Borderland." *Identities*, 4(2), 245–280. DOI: 10.1080/1070289X.1997.9962590

Ford, Rochelle, Sara Gonzales and Victoria Quade. 2020. "Collaborative and Inclusive Journalism: More Than Words." *Journalism & Mass Communication Educator*, 75(1), 58–63. DOI: 10.1177/1077695819900740

Foucault, Michel. 1972. *The Archaeology of Knowledge*. New York, NY: Routledge.

Fresh Air. 2003. "Professor and Writer Azar Nafisi." *NPR*, April 4, 2003. https://www w.npr.org/templates/story/story.php?storyId=1218984

Fuchs, Christian. 2012. "Behind the News: Social Media, Riots, and Revolutions." *Capital and Class*, 36(3), 383–391. DOI: 10.1177/0309816812453613

Gans, Herbert J. 2011. "Multiperspectival News Revisited: Journalism and Representative Democracy." *Journalism*, 12(1), 3–13. DOI: 10.1177/1464884910385289

Geiger, A. W. 2019. "Key Findings about the Online News Landscape in America." *Pew Research*, September 11, 2019. https://www.pewresearch.org/fact-tank/2019 /09/11/key-findings-about-the-online-news-landscape-in-america/

Gelvin, James L. 2017. *The New Middle East: What Everyone Needs to Know*. Oxford University Press.

Gerbaudo, Paolo and Emiliano Treré. 2015. "In Search of the 'We' of Social Media Activism: Introduction to the Special Issue on Social Media and Protest Identities." *Information, Communication and Society*, 18(8), 1–7. DOI: 10.1080/1369118X.2015.1043319

Gerstein, Josh and Jeremy C. F. Lin. 2018. "Why These 7 Countries are Listed on Trump's Travel Ban." *Politico*, June 26, 2018. https://www.politico.com/interactiv es/2018/trump-travelban-supreme-court-decision-countries-map/

Gheytanchi, Elham and Valetine N. Moghada. 2014. "Women, Social Protests, and the New Media Activism in the Middle East and North Africa." *International Review of Modern Sociology*, 40(1), 1–26. https://www.jstor.org/stable/43496487

Gholami, Niloofar. [@NilooGholami]. 2018. *Iranian Women and Iranian FeministsAre NOT on the Same Side with Islam Apologists like @lsarsour. Islam and Sharia law*. Twitter, January 18, 2018. https://twitter.com/NilooGholami/st atus/954034358087770112

Gilligan, Carol. 1982. *In a Different Voice: Psychological Theory and Women's Development*. Cambridge, MA: Harvard University Press.

Giorgis, Hannah. 2019. "The Faulty Logic in Trump's Travel Ban." *The Atlantic*, January 13, 2019. https://www.theatlantic.com/politics/archive/2019/01/trumps-travel-ban-logicflaw/579631/

Gitlin, Todd. 1980. *The Whole World is Watching: Mass Media in the Making & Unmaking of the New Left*. Berkeley: University of California Press.

Gladstone, Rick. 2019. "She Defended Iranian Women Who Removed Their Head Coverings. Now She is a Convict." *New York Times*, March 6, 2019. https://www.nyt imes.com/2019/03/06/world/middleeast/nasrin-sotoudeh-iran-head-covering.html

Gökariksel, Banu and Sara Smith. 2017. "Intersectional Feminism Beyond U.S. FlagHijab and Pussy Hats in Trump's American." *Gender, Place & Culture*, 5, 628–644. DOI: 10.1080/0966369X.2017.1343284

Golden Wheat Sami. [@goldenwheatsami]. 2019. *It's None of Your Business/ Youaren't My Voice and My Nation's Voice/So Plz Be Silence.* Twitter, February 5, 2019.twitter.com/Goldenwheatsami/status/1092674307745026048

Gozari, Golriz. [@GolrizGozari]. 2019. *Nonsense !!!!!!!!! With This Card You Have ALot to Question. The Prime Minister of New Zealand Actually Displayed a Form.* Twitter, March 26, 2019. twitter.com/golrizgozari/status/1110713084463636480

Graham-Harrison, Emma. 2019. "Saudi Arabia Allows Women to Travel Without Male Guardian's Approval." *The Guardian*, August 1, 2019. https://www.theguard ian.com/world/2019/aug/01/saudi-women-can-now-travel-without-a-male-guardia n-reports-say

Grewal, Inderpal and Caren Kaplan. 1994. *Scattered Hegemonies: Postmodernity and Transnational Feminist Practices.* Minneapolis, MN: University of Minneapolis Press.

Hafez, Kai. 2009. "Let's Improve 'Global Journalism'!" *Journalism, 10*(3), 329–331. DOI: 10.1177/1464884909102576

Hallin, Daniel C. 2009. "Not the End of Journalism History." *Journalism, 10*(3), 332–334. DOI: 10.1177/1464884909102593

Hamdy, Naila. 2009. "Arab Citizen Journalism in Action: Challenging Mainstream Media, Authorities and Media Laws." *Westminster Papers in Communication and Culture, 6*(1), 92–112. DOI:10.16997/wpcc.110

Hamidaddin, Abdullah. 2014. "Remembering Fouad Ajami, the Realist Arab." *Al Arabiya*, June 27, 2014. https://english.alarabiya.net/views/news/middle-east/2014 /06/27/Remembering-Foud-Ajami-the-realist-Arab

Harlow, Summer and Thomas J. Johnson. "The Arab Spring: Overthrowing the Protest Paradigm? How The New York Times, Global Voices and Twitter Covered the Egyptian Revolution." *International Journal of Communication, 5*, 1359–1374.

Harvard, Sarah. 2018. "8 Iranian Women Want You to Know What It Really Meansto Not Wear the Hijab." *Upworthy*, January 31, 2018. https://www.upworthy.com/8 -iranian-women-want-you-to-know-what-it-really-means-to-not-wear-the-hijab

Harvey, David. 2005. *A Brief History of Neoliberalism.* Oxford University Press.

Hasan, Md Mahmudul. 2018. "The Feminist "Quarantine" on Hijab: A Study of Its Two Mutually Exclusive Sets of Meanings." *Muslim Minority Affairs, 38*(1), 24–38. DOI: 10.1080/13602004.2018.1434941

Hatef, Azeta and Rose Luqiu. 2020. "Media and Intervention: Examining Representations of Afghan Women in *The New York Times*." *Journalism Practice*, 1–16. DOI: https://doi.org/10.1080/17512786.2020.1749110

Hawkesworth, Mary E. 2006. *Globalization & Feminist Activism.* Maryland: Rowman & Littlefield.

Heath, Jennifer. 2008. *The Veil: Women Writers on Its History, Lore, and Politics.* Berkeley: University of California Press.

Hedge, Radha Sarma. 2011. *Circuits of Visibility: Gender and Transnational Media Cultures.* NYU Press.

Heim, Kyle. 2021. "Tweets and Source Diversity: Newspapers' Sourcing of Twitter Posts from 2009 to 2016." *Mass Communication and Society.* https://doi.org/10.1 080/15205436.2021.1883063

Hellmueller, Lea. 2017. "Gatekeeping Beyond Geographical Borders: Developing and Analytical Model of Transnational Journalism Cultures." *The International Communication Gazette, 79*(1), 3–25. DOI: 10.1177/1748048516656304

Hellmueller, Lea, Sadia A. Cheema and Xu Zhang. 2017. "The Networks of Global Journalism: Global News Construction Through the Collaboration of Global News Startups with Freelancers." *Journalism Studies, 18*(1), 45–64. DOI: 10.1080/1461670X.2016.1215254

Helmore, Edward. 2017. "Munira Ahmed: The Woman Who Became the Face of theTrump Resistance." *The Guardian*, January 23, 2017. https://www.theguardian.com/us-news/2017/jan/23/womens-march-poster-munira-ahmed-shepard-fairey-interview

Herman, Edward S. 1993. "The Media's Role in U.S. Foreign Policy." *Journal of International Affairs, 47*(*1*), 24–45. https://www.jstor.org/stable/24357083

Hermida, Alfred. 2010. "Twittering the News." *Journalism Practice, 4*(3), 297–308. DOI: 10.1080/17512781003640703

Hermida, Alfred. 2013. "#Journalism." *Digital Journalism, 1*(3), 295–313. DOI:10.1080/21670811.2013.808456

Hermida, Alfred, Seth C. Lewis and Rodrigo Zamith. 2014. "Sourcing the Arab Spring: A Case Study of Andy Carvin's Sources on Twitter During the Tunisian and Egyptian Revolutions." *Journal of Computer-Mediated Communication, 19*(3), 479–499. DOI: 10.1111/jcc4.12074

Herr, Ranjoo Seodu. 2014. "Reclaiming Third World Feminism: or Why Transnational Feminism Needs Third World Feminism." *Meridians: Feminism, Race, Transnationalism, 12*(1), 1–30. DOI: 10.2979/meridians.12.1.1

Hjelmgaard, Kim. 2018. "In Iran, Most Women Must Live as Second-Class Citizens, But Some are Making Strides." *USA Today*, August 30, 2018. https://amp.usatoday.com/amp/1131193002

Hmg. [@Hmg60671352]. 2019. *@AlinejadMasih Why Do You Think You Can Talk OnBehalf of Iranian People? Just Because of the Number of Your*. Twitter, May 10, 2019.twitter.com/Hmg60671352/status/1127070078149844993

Hodges, Julie. 2017. "Cracking the Walls of Leadership: Women in Saudi Arabia." *Gender in Management: An International Journal, 32*(1), 34–46. DOI: 10.1108/GM-11-2015-0106

Hoover Institution. n.d. "Ayaan Hirsi Ali." Accessed March 26, 2021. https://www.hoover.org/profiles/ayaan-hirsi-ali

Holt, Maria and H. A. Jawad. 2013. *Women, Islam, and Resistance in the Arab World*. Boulder, CO: Lynne Rienner Publishers Inc.

Human Rights Foundation. n.d. "Masih Alinejad: Iranian Journalist and Activist." Accessed March 26, 2021. *Human Rights Foundation*. https://hrf.org/event_speakers_posts/masih-alinejad/

Hossain, Mohammad Delwar and James. 2017. "The Ethics of Care as a Universal Framework for Global Journalism. *Journal of Media Ethics, 33*(4), 198–211. DOI: 10.1080/23736992.2018.1509713

Ibrahim, Dina. 2009. "Framing of Arab Countries on American News Networks Following the September 11 Attacks." *Journal of Arab & Muslim Research, 1*(3), 279–296. DOI: 10.1386/jammr.1.3.279_1

Ingber, Sasha. 2018. "'Vogue' Cover of Saudi Princess in the Driver's Seat Sparks Controversy." *NPR*, June 1, 2018. https://www.npr.org/sections/thetwo-way/2018/06/01/616077816/vogue-cover-of-saudi-princess-in-the-drivers-seat-sparks-controversy

Iyengar, Shanto. 1991. *Is Anyone Responsible? How Television Frames Political Issues*. Chicago: University of Chicago Press.

James, Paul. 2005. "Arguing Globalizations: Propositions towards an Investigation of Global Formation." *Globalizations*, 2(2), 193–209. DOI: 10.1080/14747730500202206

Jaquette, Jane S. 2011. "Women and Modernization Theory: A Decade of Feminist Criticism." *World Politics*, 32(2), 267–284. DOI: 10.2307/2010265

Jorgensen, Marianne and Louise J. Phillips. 2002. *Discourse Analysis as Theory and Method*. London: Sage Publications.

Kechichian, Joseph A. 2014. "A 'Rare' Arab Intellectual: Fouad Ajami (1945–2014)."*Al Jazeera*, June 24, 2014. https://www.aljazeera.com/opinions/2014/6/24/a-rare-arab-intellectual-fouad-ajami-1945-2014

Keck, Margaret E. and Kathryn Sikkink. 2014. *Activists Beyond Borders: Advocacy Networks in International Politics*. Ithaca, NY: Cornell University Press.

Keddie, Nikki. 2007. *Women in the Middle East: Past and Present*. Princeton and Oxford: Princeton University Press.

Kennedy, Merrit and Jackie Northam. 2020. "Was it Legal for the U.S. to Kill A TopIranian Military Leader?" *NPR*, January 4, 2020. https://www.npr.org/2020/01/04/793412105/was-it-legal-for-the-u-s-to-kill-a-top-iranian-military-leader

Khamiaze. [@Khamiaze]. 2018. *@AlinejadMasih and @FedericaMog Consider Giving An Interview to An #Italian magazine about Masih Alinejad Who Betrays #Iranian People, Men and*. Twitter, July 7, 2018. twitter.com/khamiaze/status/1015473608934772736

Khondker, Habibul Haque. 2011. "Role of the New Media in the Arab Spring." *Globalizations*, 8(5), 675–679. DOI: 10.1080/14747731.2011.621287

Khosravinik, Majid and Nadia Sarkhoh. 2017. "Arabism and Anti-Persian Sentiments on Participatory Web Platforms: A Social Media Critical Discourse Study." *International Journal of Communication*, 11, 3614–3633.

Kianpour, Suzanne. 2015. "Iran Negotiations: The Women Who Made the Iran Nuclear Deal Happen." *BBC News*. August 6, 2015. https://www.bbc.com/news/world-us-canada-33728879

Kim, Jang Hyun, Su, Tuo-Yu and Hong Junhao. 2007. "The Influence of Geopolitics and Foreign Policy on the U.S. and Canadian Media: An Analysis of Newspaper Coverage of Sudan's Darfur Conflict." *The International Journal of Press/Politics*, 12(3), 87–95. DOI: 10.1177/1081180X07302972

Konieczna, Magda, Kristine Mattis, Jiun-Yi Tsai, Xuan Liang and Sharon Dunwoody. 2014."Global Journalism in Decision-Making Moments: A Case Study of Canadian and American Television Coverage of the 2009 United Nations Framework Convention on Climate Change in Copenhagen." *Environmental Communication*, 8(4), 489–507. DOI: 10.1080/17524032.2014.909509

Kotz, David M. 2002. "Globalization and Neoliberalism." *Rethinking Marxism*, *14*(2), 64–79. DOI: 10.1080/089356902101242189

Kumar, Deepa. 2018. "The Right Kind of "Islam": News Media Representations of US-Saudi Relations During the Cold War." *Journalism Studies*, *19*(8), 1079–1097. DOI:10.1080/1461670X.2016.1259012

Lalami, L. 2006. "The Missionary Position." *The Nation*, June 1, 2006. https://www .thenation.com/article/archive/missionary-position/

Lawless, Brandi and Chen, Yea-Wen. 2016. "Reclaiming their Historical Agency": A Critical Analysis of International News Discourse on Occupy and Arab Spring." *Howard Journal of Communications*, *27*(3), 185–202. DOI: 10.1080/10646175.2016.1156591

Lee, Latoya A. 2017. "Black Twitter: A Response to Bias in Mainstream Media." *Social Sciences*, *6*(26), 1–17. DOI: 10.3390/socsci6010026

Lee, Paul S. N., Clement Y. K. So and Louis Leung. 2015. "Social Media and Umbrella Movement: Insurgent Public Sphere in Formation." *Chinese Journal of Communication*, *8*(4), 356–375. DOI: 10.1080/17544750.2015.1088874

Levs, Josh. 2012. "Fact Check: Was Obama 'Silent' on Iran 2009 Protests?" *CNN*, October 9, 2012. https://www.cnn.com/2012/10/08/politics/fact-check-romney-ir an/index.html

Lievrouw, Leah A. 2011. *Alternative and Activist New Media*. Cambridge, MA: Polity.

Lim, Merlyna. 2018. "Unveiling Saudi Feminism(s): Historicization, Heterogeneity, and Corporeality in Women's Movements." *Canadian Journal of Communication*, *43*, 461–479. DOI: 10.22230/cjc.2018v43n3a3379

Lindell, Johan and Michael Karlsson. 2016. "Cosmopolitan Journalists? Global Journalism in the Work and Visions of Journalists." *Journalism Studies*, *17*(7), 860–970. DOI: 10.1080/1461670X.2016.1165137

Loker, Jessica. 2019. *Fox News Sunday*. October 13, 2019. Washington, DC: Fox News Network.

Lowery, Wesley. 2020. "A Reckoning Over Objectivity, Led by Black Journalists." *New York Times*, June 23, 2020. https://www.nytimes.com/2020/06/23/opinion/ob jectivity-black-journalists-coronavirus.html

MacCallum, Martha. 2018. *The Story with Martha MacCallum*. August 9, 2018. New York City: Fox News Network.

MacCallum, Martha. 2020. *The Story with Martha MacCallum*. January 10, 2018. New York City: Fox News Network.

Mahmood, Saba. 2003. "Ethical Formation and Politics of Individual Autonomy in Contemporary Egypt." *Social Research*, *70*(3), 837–866. https://www.jstor.org/ stable/40971643

Mahmood, Saba. 2011. *Politics of Piety: The Islamic Revival and the Feminist Subject*. New Jersey: Princeton University Press.

Malik, Nesrine. 2018. "Islam's New 'Native Informants.'" *The New York Review of Books*, June 7, 2018. https://www.nybooks.com/daily/2018/06/07/islams-new-nat ive-informants/?lp_txn_id=1007243

Marral(a). [@sham_marral]. 2019. *No, Vogue is Pro-Women's* Choice@ AlinejadMasih. *Your Islamophobic Feminism Cosies Up to the Far-Right, Denies HijabiWomen Agency.* Twitter, March 30, 2019. https://twitter.com/sham_marral/status/1112099840966692865

Marral(b). [@sham_marral]. 2019. *The Anti-Compulsory Hijab Movement is Important in Iran. But to Suggest that Hijabi Women in the West (Or Even).* Twitter, March 30, 2019. twitter.com/sham_marral/status/1112102340914569223

Martin, Douglas. 2014. "Fouad Ajami, Commentator and Expert in Arab History, Dies at 68." *New York Times*, June 22, 2014. https://www.nytimes.com/2014/06/23/us/fouad-ajami-is-dead-at-68-expert-in-arab-history.html

Martin, Douglas. 2018. "Bernard Lewis, Influential Scholar of Islam, Is Dead at 101." *New York Times*, May 21, 2018. https://nyti.ms/2IWw06E

Marks, Monica, L. 2012. "Do Arabs Really 'Hate' Women? The Problem with Native Informants." *The Huffington Post*, June 25, 2012. https://www.huffpost.com/entry/doarabs-really-hate-wome_b_1453147

Marx, Karl and Friedrich Engels. 1955. *The Communist Manifesto.* Wiley-Blackwell (1602).

McCluskey, Molly. 2017. "Inaugural Protest Poster Stirs Debate among Muslim American Women." *Middle East Eye*, January 20, 2017. https://www.middleasteye.net/news/inaugural-protest-poster-stirs-debate-among-muslim-american-women

McGinty, Anna Mansson. 2014. "Emotional Geographies of Veiling: The Meanings of the Hijab for Five Palestinian American Muslim Women." *Gender, Place and Culture, 21*(6), 683–700. DOI: 10.1080/0966369X.2013.810601

McLaughlin, Lisa. 2007. "Transnational Feminism and the Revolutionary Association of the Women of Afghanistan." In *Media on the Move: Global Flow and Contra-Flow,* edited by D. K. Thusu, 221–236. New York City, NY: Routledge.

McLuhan, Marshall. (1967). *The Medium is the Message: An Inventory of Effects.* London: Penguin Press.

Mehrzad. [@mehrza]. 2018. *@AlinejadMasih and @FedericaMog Maybe You Should First Tell That "Italian" Magazine How You Managed to Become a (Paid To Play).* Twitter, July 6, 2018. twitter.com/mehrza/status/1015212935340265473

Meynoosh. [@meynooshh]. 2018. *You are #Fake_ Feminist and Sinister Muslim. InIran Women are Aware and Know You and Islamic Terrorism. #BackOffLinda.* Twitter, January 18, 2018. https://twitter.com/meynooshh/status/954038670750830592

Miller, David. 1999. "Bounded Citizenship." In *Cosmopolitan Citizenship*, edited by Roland Dannreuther and Kimberly Hutchings, 60–80. New York: Palgrave Macmillan.

Miller, Stephen L. 2018. "Women are Leading in Iran: Where is their Voice of Support From the Left?" *Fox News*, January 2, 2018. https://www.foxnews.com/opinion/women-are-leading-in-iran-where-is-their-voice-of-support-from-the-left

Mishra, Smeeta. 2007. "Liberation" vs. "Purity": Representations of Saudi Women in the American Press and American Press and American Women in the

Saudi Press." *The Howard Journal of Communications*, *18*, 259–276. DOI: 10.1080/10646170701490849

Mislán, Cristina and Dache-Gerbino, Amalia. 2018. "The Struggle for 'Our Streets': The Digital and Physical Spatial Politics of the Ferguson Movement." *Social Movement Studies*, *17*(6), 676–696. DOI: 10.1080/14742837.2018.1533810

Mislán, Cristina and Shaban, Sara. 2018. "To Ferguson, Love Palestine": Mediating Life under Occupation. *Communication and Critical/Cultural Studies*, *16*(1), 43–60. DOI:10.1080/14791420.2019.1594325

Moallam, Minoo, Caren Kaplan and Norma Alarcón. 1999. *Between Woman and Nation: Nationalisms, Transnational Feminisms, and the State*. Durham and London: Duke University Press.

Moaveni, Azadeh. 2018. "How the Trump Administration is Exploiting Iran's Burgeoning Feminist Movement." *The New Yorker*, July 9, 2018. https://www.newyorker.com/news/news-desk/how-the-trump-administration-isexploiting-irans-burgeoning-feminist-movement

Moghadam, Valentine M. 2000. "Transnational Feminist Networks: Collective Action in an Era of Globalization." *International Sociology*, *15*(1), 57–85. DOI: 10.1177/0268580900015001004

Moghadam, Valentine M. and Fatima Sadiqi. 2006. "Women and the Public Sphere in the Middle East and North Africa: Introduction and Overview." Introduction to Special Issue. *Journal of Middle East Women's Studies*, *2*(2, Spring), 1–7.

Mohanty, Chandra Talpade. 2003. *Feminism without Borders: Decolonizing Theory, Practicing Solidarity*. Durham, NC: Duke University Press.

Mohanty, Chandra Talpade. 1988. "Under Western Eyes: Feminist Scholarship and Colonial Discourses." *Feminist Review*, *30*(1), 61–88.

Mtango, Sifa. 2004. "A State of Oppression? Women's Rights in Saudi Arabia." *Asia-Pacific Journal on Human Rights and the Law 1*, 49–67. DOI: 10.1163/1571815043075166

Murrell, Colleen. 2014. *Foreign Correspondents and International Newsgathering: The Role of Fixers*. England, UK: Routledge.

Musto, Julia. 2020. "Iranian Activist Masih Alinejad: The People of Iran Did Not Mourn Qassem Soleimani's Death." *Fox News*, January 3, 2020. https://www.foxnews.com/media/iranian-journalist-reacts-qassem-soleimani-airstrike-death

Myers, Garth, Klak, Thomas and Timothy Koehl. 1996. "The Inscription of Difference: News Coverage of the Conflicts in Rwanda and Bosnia." *Political Geography*, *15*(1), 21–46. DOI: 10.1016/0962-6298(95)00041-0

Nafisi, Azar. n.d. "Azar Nafisi." Accessed on March 26, 2021. https://azarnafisi.com/about-azar/Naghibi, Nima. 2007. *Rethinking Global Sisterhood: Western Feminism and Iran*. Minneapolis: London.

Nazanin. [Nazaninmrzn]. 2019. @*AlinejadMasih and @SecPompeo It Was Definitely the Best News These Days. Masih [sic] Has Always Been and Still Is The.* Twitter, February 4, 2019. twitter.com/Nazaninmrzn/status/1092463081886748673)

[@ninianomada]. 2019. Twitter, May 13, 2019. https://twitter.com/ninianomada/status/1127945974507196416

O'Brien, Timothy L. 2018. "Look Who's Not in Trump's Travel Ban." *Bloomberg*, June 26,2018. https://www.bloomberg.com/opinion/articles/2018-06-26/trump-travel-ban-doesnt-cover-saudi-arabia-or-the-u-a-e

O'Tuathail, Gearoid. 1996. "An Anti-Geopolitical Eye: Maggie O'Kane in Bosnia, 1992–93."*Gender, Place and Culture: A Journal of Feminist Geography, 3*(2), 171–186. DOI: 10.1080/09663699650021873

Palladino, Robert. 2019. "Secretary Pompeo's Meeting with Iranian Women's Rights Activist Masih Alinejad." *U.S. Virtual Embassy Iran*, February 4, 2019. https://ir.usembassy.gov/secretary-pompeos-meeting-with-iranian-womens-rights-activist-masih-alinejad/

Papacharissi, Zizi. "Affective Publics and Structures of Storytelling: Sentiment, Events and Mediality." *Information, Communication & Society, 19*(3), 307–324. DOI: 10.1080/1369118X.2015.1109697.

Papacharissi, Zizi and Oliveira, Maria de Fatima. 2012. "Affective News and Networked Publics: The Rhythms of News Storytelling on #Egypt." *Journal of Communication, 62*(2), 266–282. DOI: 10.1111/j.1460-2466.2012.01630.

Pennington, Rosemary and Birthisel, Jessica. 2015. "When New Media Make News: Framing Technology and Assault in the Stuebenville Rape Case." *New Media & Society, 18*(11), 2435–2451. DOI: 10.1177/1461444815612407

Plaut, Shayna and Klein, Peter. 2019. "'Fixing' the Journalist-Fixer Relationship: A Critical Look Towards Developing Best Practices in Global Reporting." *Journalism Studies, 20*(12), 1696–1713. DOI: 10.1080/1461670X.2019.1638292

Powell, Kimberly A. 2011. "Framing Islam: An Analysis of U.S. Media Coverage of Terrorism Since 9/11." *Communication Studies, 62*(1), 90–112. DOI: 10.1080/10510974.2011.533599

Radio Farda. 2019. "Pompeo Tells Iranian Rights Activist of U.S. Support." *Radio Farda*, February 5, 2019. https://en.radiofarda.com/a/pompeo-meets-with-alinejad-and-voicesus-support/29752266.html

Rafat, Ahmad. 2019. "After Meeting Pompeo, Iranian Activist Masih Alinejad Speaksto Kayhan Life." *Kayhan Life*, February 7, 2019. https://kayhanlife.com/pe ople/after-meeting-pompeo-iranian-activist-masih-alinejad-speaks-to-kayhan-life/

Rahbari, Ladan. 2019. "Gender, Sexuality and the Moral Body: A Qualitative Study of Perceptions and Experiences of Body Management among Women in Iran and Iranian Migrant Women in Belgium." http://hdl.handle.net/1854/LU-8617088

Rahbari, Ladan. 2020. "When Gender Turns Right: Racializing Islam and Femonationalism in Online Political Discourses in Belgium." *Contemporary Politics, 27*(1), 41–57. https://doi.org/10.1080/13569775.2020.1813950

Rahman, Bushra. 2007. "Images of Muslim Women in International Magazines: A Case of *Time* and *Newsweek 1979–2002*." Unpublished PhD thesis, Institute of Communication Studies, University of the Punjab.

Ranani, Saied Reza Ameli and Kharazmi, Zoreh Nosrat. 2017. "The Significance of Muslim Women in American Foreign Policy Case Study: Hillary Clinton's Prophecy for Women of Science in MENA." *Women's Studies International Forum, 61*, 20–27. DOI: 10.1016/j.wsif.2016.12.006

Rao, Shakuntala and Lee, Seow T. 2005. "Globalizing Media Ethics: An Assessment of Universal Ethics Among International Political Journalists." *Journal of Mass Media Ethics, 20*(2&3), 99–120. DOI: 10.1080/08900523.2005.9679703

Reese, Stephen D. 2010. "Journalism and Globalization." *Sociology Compass*, 344–353. DOI: 10.1111/j.1751-9020.2010.00282.x

Reese, Stephen D. and Lewis, Seth C. 2009. "Framing the War on Terror: The Internalization of Policy in the US Press." *Journalism, 10*, 777–797. DOI: 10.1177/1464884909344480

Reisigl, Martin and Ruth Wodak. 2009. "The Discourse-Historical Approach (DHA)." In *Methods of Critical Discourse Analysis*, edited by Ruth Wodak and Michael Meyer, 2nd ed., 87–121. London, UK: SAGE Publications.

Repucci, Sarah. 2019. "Media Freedom: A Downward Spiral." *Freedom House*. https://freedomhouse.org/report/freedom-and-media/2019/media-freedom-downward-spiral

Reyes, Giovanni E. 2001. "Four Main Theories of Development: Modernization, Dependency, Word-System, and Globalization." *Nomadas. Revista Critica de Ciencias Sociales y Juridicas, 4*, 1–16.

Rich, Adrienne. 1984. "Notes towards a Politics of Location." In *Feminist Postcolonial Theory: A Reader,* edited by Reina Lewis and Sara Mills, 29–42. London: Routledge.

Riker, William H. 1986. *The Art of Political Manipulation*. New Haven: Yale University Press.

Roja. [@mathcolorstress]. 2017. *I'm an Iranian-American Feminist and against the Forced Hijab in Iran and I Support @lsarsour. The Women's March and.* Twitter, December 31, 2017. https://twitter.com/mathcolorstrees/status/94765854 0453265408

Sahimi, Muhammad. 2010. "Iranian Women and the Struggle for Democracy." *Frontline*, April 15, 2010. https://www.pbs.org/wgbh/pages/frontline/tehranbur eau/2010/04/iranian-women-and-the-struggle-for-democracy-i-the-pre-revolution -era.html

Said, Edward. 1978. *Orientalism*. New York: Vintage Books.

Said, Edward. 1981. *Covering Islam*. New York: Pantheon.

Said, Edward. 2003. "The Academy of Lagado: The US Administration's Misguided War." *London Book Review*, April 17, 2003. https://www.lrb.co.uk/the-paper/v25/ n08/edward-said/the-academy-of-lagado

Sakr, Naomi. 2008. "Women and Media in Saudi: Rhetoric, Reductionism and Realities." *British Journal of Middle Eastern Studies, 33*(3), 385–404. DOI: 10.1080/13530190802525197

Salat, H. [@halimasalat]. 2020. *There is No Comparison Between These Two Women. One Has Principles, Integrity & Is a Passionate Advocate for Freedom At.* Twitter, January 10, 2020. https://twitter.com/halimasalat/status/1215685387856875520

Salim, Mustafa, Missy Ryan, Liz Sly John Hudson. 2020. "In Major Escalation, American Strike Kills Top Iranian Commander in Baghdad." *Washington Post*, January 2, 2020. https://www.washingtonpost.com/world/national-security/defen se-secretary-says-iran-and-its-proxies-may-be-planning-fresh-attacks-on-us-perso nnel-in-iraq/2020/01/02/53b63f00-2d89-11ea-bcb3-ac6482c4a92f_story.html

Sameh, Catherine. 2010. "Discourses of Equality, Rights and Islam in the One Million Signatures Campaign in Iran." *International Feminist Journal of Politics*, *12*(3), 444–463. DOI: 10.1080/14616742.2010.513113

Sanger, David E. 2020. "For Trump, A Risky Gamble to Deter Iran." *New York Times*, January 3,2020. https://nyti.ms/2SSwAqD

Sarsour, Linda. [@lsarsour]. 2019. *Nothing is More Dangerous and Threatening to Powerful Men Than a Bold Woman Who Defends Other Women. This Is a.* Twitter, March 12, 2019. https://twitter.com/lsarsour/status/1105639466683822083

Schudson, Michael. 2011. *The Sociology of News*. W.W. Norton & Company.

Scott, Katy. 2018. *CNN Wire*. February 17, 2018. Atlanta, GA: CNN.

Seddighi, Gilda and Sara Tafakori. 2016. "Transnational Mediation of State Gendered Violence: The Case of Iran." *Feminist Media Studies*, *16*(5), 925–928. DOI: 10.1080/14680777.2016.1213575

Shahbaz, Adrian. 2019. "Why Social Media Are Still Worth Saving." *Freedom House*. https://freedomhouse.org/report/freedom-and-media/2019/media-freedom -downward-spiral

Shahrabi, Shima. 2019. "Campaigner and Journalist Masih Alinejad's Meeting with Mike Pompeo." *Iran Wire*, February 6, 2019. https://iranwire.com/en/features/5832

Shariatmadari, M. [@Maryamshariatm]. 2019. *Nasrin Sotoudeh was My Attorney after I Got Beaten & Arrested b/c of Protesting against #ShariaLaw & Mandatory Hijab. In.* Twitter, March 13, 2019. twitter.com/Maryamshariatm/status/11059305 00265439232

Shatz, Adam. 2003. "The Native Informant." *The Nation*, April 10, 2003. https://ww w.thenation.com/article/archive/native-informant/

Shoemaker, Pamela and Reese, Stephen. D. 2014. *Mediating the Message in the 21st Century: A Media Sociology Perspective*. New York, NY: Routledge.

Shome, Raka. 2006. "Transnational Feminism and Communication Studies." *The Communication Review 9*, 255–267. DOI: 10.1080/10714420600957266

Siddiqi, Dina Mahnaz. 2011. "Islam, Gender and the Nation: The Social Life of Bangladeshi Fatwas." In *Communalism and Globalization in South Asia and its Diaspora (Intersections: Colonial and Postcolonial Histories)*, edited by Deana Heath and Chandana Mathur, 181–203. New York: Routledge.

Sigal, Leon V. 1973. *Reporters and Officials: The Organization and Politics of News Making*. Lexington: Massachusetts: D.C. Heath and Company

Silverman, Craig. 2011. "Is this the World's Best Twitter account? Columbia Journalism Review." April 8, 2011. http://www.cjr.org/behind_the_news/is_this _the_worlds_best_twitter_account.php

Sima, S. [@SalmanSima]. 2019. *Nasrin Sotoudeh Advocates Human Rights. Attorney of Women Prosecuted in Iran for Opposing Mandatory Hijab. She Bravely Defended Them. She.* Twitter, March 13, 2019.

Smith, Candace. 2016. "Donald Trump Says He'll Consider Replacing Hijab-Wearing TSA Agents with Veterans." *ABC News*, July 1, 2016. https://abcnews.go.com/Po litics/donald-trumprequest-rally-goer-replacehijab-wearing/story?id=40269164

Smith, Jordan Michael. 2019. "How Voice of America Persian Became a Trump Administration PR Machine." *The Intercept*, August 13, 2019. https://theintercept .com/2019/08/13/trump-voa-persian/

Snyder, R. Claire. 2008. "What is Third-Wave feminism? A New Directions Essay." *Signs: Journal of Women in Culture and Society, 34*(1), 175–196. DOI: 10.1086/588436

Sreberny, Annabelle and Gholam Khiabany. 2010. *Blogistan: The Internet and Politics in Iran.* New York, NY: I. B. Tauris.

Steiner, Linda. 2018. "Solving Journalism's Post-Truth Crisis with Feminist Standpoint Theory." *Journalism Studies,* 1–12. DOI: 10. 1080/1461670X.2018.1498749

Steiner, Linda and Chad M. Okrusch. 2011. "Care as a Virtue for Journalists." *Journal of Mass Media Ethics, 21*(2&3), 102–122. DOI: 10.1080/08900523.2006.9679728

Stephan, Rita. 2013. "Cyberfeminism and Its Political Implications for Women in the Arabworld." *E-International Relations,* August 28, 2013. https://www.e-ir.info/201 3/08/28/cyberfeminism-and-its-political-implications-for-women-in-the-arab-world/

Tamasha. [@Tamaashaaa]. 2018. *@AlinejadMasih @kargadan and @ FedericaMogWould You Please Stop Advocating for the People You Yourself Betrayed at the First Place? We.* Twitter, July 7, 2018. twitter.com/Tamaashaaa/st atus/1015626197458399233

Taylor, Michael and Kanso, Heba. 2019. "New Zealand Women Face Praise and Protests for Donning the Hijab." *Reuters,* March 26, 2019. https://www.reuters. com/article/us-newzealand-shootout-headscarves/new-zealand-women-face-praise -and-protests-for-donning-the-hijab-idUSKCN1R71Q9

Terman, Rochelle. 2017. "Islamophobia and Media Portrayals of Muslim Women: A Computational Text Analysis of US News Coverage." *International Studies Quarterly, 61,* 489–502. DOI: 10.1093/isq/sqx051

Thorsen, Einar and Chindu Sreedharan. 2019. "#EndMaleGuardianship: Women's Rights, Social Media and the Arab Public Sphere." *New Media & Society, 21*(5), 1121–1140. DOI: 10.177/146144818821376

Tinati, Ramine, Susan Halford, Leslie Carr, and Catherine Pope. 2014. "Big Data: Methodological Challenges and Approaches for Sociological Analysis." *Sociology, 48*(4), 663–681. DOI: 10.1177/0038038513511561

Tipps, Dean, C. 1976. "Modernization Theory and the Comparative Study of Societies: A Critical Perspective." In *Comparative Modernization: A Reader,* edited by in Cyril E. Black. 62–88. New York: Free Press.

Tisdall, Simon. 2009. "When will Obama Back Persian People Power?" *The Guardian,* June 17, 2009. https://www.theguardian.com/commentisfree/cifamerica /2009/jun/17/barack-obama-iran-protests

Tohidi, Nayereh. 2016. "The Women's Movement and Feminism in Iran: Revisiting a Global Perspective." In *Women's Movements in the Global Era,* edited by AmritaBasu, 2nd ed., 397–442. Boulder, CO: Westview Press.

Topal, Aylin. 2019. "Economic Reforms and Women's Empowerment in Saudi Arabia." *Women's Studies International Forum, 76,* 1–8. DOI: 10.1016/j. wsif.2019.102253

Tronto, Joan. 1995. "Care as a Basis for Radical Political Judgements." *Hypatia, 10*(2), 141–149.

Tufekci, Zeynep, and Christopher Wilson. 2012. "Social Media and the Decision to Participate in Political Protest: Observations from Tahrir Square." *Journal of Communication, 62*(2), 363–379. DOI: 10.1111/j.1460-2466.2012.01629.x

U.S. Virtual Embassy Iran. 2019. "Secretary Pompeo's Meeting with Iranian Women's Rights Activist Masih Alinejad." February 4, 2019. https://ir.usem bassy.gov/secretary-pompeos-meeting-with-iranian-womens-rights-activist-masih -alinejad/

Valoy, Patricia. 2015. "Transnational Feminism: Why Feminist Activism Needs to Think Globally." *Everyday Feminism*, January 28, 2015. https://everydayfemi nism.com/2015/01/why-we-need-transnational-feminism/

Vanacker, Bastiaan and John Breslin. 2011. "Ethics of Care: More Than Just Another Tool to Bash the Media?" *Journal of Mass Media Ethics*, *21*(2–3), 196–214. DOI: 10.1080/08900523.2006.9679733

van der Haak, Bregtje, Parks, Michael and Castells, Manuel. 2012. "The Future of Journalism: Networked Digital Age." *International Journal of Communication*, *6*, 2923–2938.

van Dijk, Teun A. 1997. "The Study of Discourse." In *Discourses as Structure and Process*, edited by Teun A, 1–34. van Dijk. London: Sage.

Van Leuven, Sarah and Peter Berglez. 2016. "Global Journalism Between Dream and Reality: AComparative Study of *The Times, Le Monde,* and *De Standard.*" *Journalism Studies*, *17*(6), 667–683. DOI: 10.1080/1461670X.2015.1017596

Vogl, Lisa. n.d. "About Us." *Verona-Collection*, March 26, 2021. https://www.ver onacollection.com/pages/about-us-1

Ward, Stephen, J. A. 2005. "Philosophical Foundations for Global Journalism Ethics." *Journal of Mass Media Ethics*, *20*(1), 3–21. DOI: 10.1207/s15327728jmme2001_2

Ward, Stephen J. A. 2010. *Global Journalism Ethics*. Montreal: McGill-Queen's University Press.

Watson, Amy. 2019. "Most Popular News Websites in the United States as of May 2018, by Unique Monthly Visitors* (In Millions)." *Statista*, August 9, 2019. https ://www.statista.com/statistics/381569/leading-news-and-media-sites-usa-by-share- of-visits/

Wells, Justin. 2018. *Tucker Carlson Tonight*. February 8, 2018. Washington, D.C.: Fox NewsNetwork.

Wells, Justin. 2019. *Tucker Carlson Tonight*. April 30, 2019. Washington, D.C.: Fox NewsNetwork.

Wingfield, Adia Harvey. 2020. "Women are Advancing in the Workplace, but Women of Colors Till Lag Behind." *Brookings*, October 2020. https://www.bro okings.edu/essay/women-are-advancing-in-the-workplace-but-women-of-color-st ill-lag-behind/

World Hijab Day. n.d. "Our Story." *World Hijab Day*, March 26, 2021. https://world- hijabday.com/our-story/

Wu, Lawrence and Michelle Lanz. 2019. "How the CIA Overthrew Iran's Democracy in 4 days." *NPR*, February 7, 2019. https://www.npr.org/2019/01/31/690363402/ how-the-cia-overthrew-irans-democracy-in-four-days

Yazdi, M. N. [@maryamnayebyazd]. 2020. *OMG. Masih Alinejad's an independent activist. She is Currently Being Attacked by Many Pro-Regime and Anti-Human Rights Forces.* Twitter, January 6, 2020. https://twitter.com/i/status/12143560114 79425024

Yuval-Davis, Nira. 2015. "Situated Intersectionality and Social Inequality." *Raisons Politiques*, 2, 91–100.

Zagor, Matthew. 2015. "The Struggle of Autonomy and Authenticity: Framing the Savage Refugee." *Social Identities*, *21*(4), 373–394. DOI: 10.1080/13504630.2015.1071702

Zayani, Mohamed. *Networked Publics and Digital Contention: The Politics of Everyday Life in Tunisia*. Oxford University Press.

Zhang, Juyan and William L. Benoit, William L. 2004. "Message Strategies of Saudi Arabia's Image Restoration Campaign after 9/11." *Public Relations Review*, *30*, 161–167. DOI: 10.1016/j.pubrev.2004.02.006

Zolqadr, Zohreh. 2020. "Iranian Women You Should Know: Zeynab Pasha." *Iran Wire*, June 7, 2020. https://iranwire.com/en/features/7135

Index

About the Author

Sara Shaban is an assistant professor of communication and journalism at Seattle Pacific University. Educated at the University of Missouri School of Journalism (PhD in journalism; media sociology) and Saint Louis University (MA in communications), Shaban identifies as a critical/cultural scholar focused on the intersections between media, women's social movements, and geopolitics in the MENA region. Shaban's academic work is rooted within the theoretical frameworks of transnationalism and femonationalism. Her research is published in the *International Journal of Communication*, *Communication and Critical Cultural Studies*, and *Journalism: Theory, Practice & Criticism*. Shaban lives in Seattle with her husband, her West Highland Terrier Amelie, and her orange cat Tito.

www.ingramcontent.com/pod-product-compliance
Lightning Source LLC
Chambersburg PA
CBHW022324280326
41932CB00010B/1218